THE
ENCHANTED
COUNTRY

THE ENCHANTED COUNTRY

Northern Writers in the South
1865–1910

ANNE ROWE

Louisiana State University Press
Baton Rouge and London

The author gratefully acknowledges permission to quote from the
following publications:

Lafcadio Hearn, *Chita: A Memory of Last Island,* University of
North Carolina Press

Lafcadio Hearn, *The Writings of Lafcadio Hearn,* 1923,
Houghton Mifflin Company.

John De Forest, *Miss Ravenel's Conversion from Secession to
Loyalty,* Charles E. Merrill Publishing Company

Henry James, *The American Scene,* Indiana University Press

Harriet Beecher Stowe, *Uncle Tom's Cabin,* Doubleday

Owen Wister, *Lady Baltimore,* Gregg Press

Owen Wister, *Roosevelt: The Story of a Friendship,* MacMillan

LIBRARY OF CONGRESS CATALOGING IN PUBLICATION DATA

Rowe, Anne, 1945-
    The enchanted country.

    Bibliography: p.
    Includes index.
    1. American fiction—19th century—History and criticism.   2.   Southern
States in literature.
I.   Title
PS377.R6   813'.4'09   78-17048
ISBN 0-8071-0453-1

To Louis D. Rubin, Jr.
whose knowledge, guidance, and patience
made this book possible
and
For Bud and Beth

Contents

Abbreviations

AS	*The American Scene*
B	*The Bostonians*
BWS	*Bricks Without Straw*
C	*Chita: A Memory of Last Island*
D	*Dred: A Tale of the Great Dismal Swamp*
FE	*A Fool's Errand*
GS	*The Great South*
LB	*Lady Baltimore*
MRC	*Miss Ravenel's Conversion from Secession to Loyalty*
PL	*Palmetto Leaves*
UTC	*Uncle Tom's Cabin*
V	*The Virginian*

Introduction

In 1873, less than a decade after the close of the Civil War, the enterprising publishers of *Scribner's Monthly* arrived at a plan designed to create interest among their readers. They commissioned a journalist, Edward King, to tour the southern states, record his observations, and from his notes supply the magazine with descriptive articles to be published serially.

King, of course, was not the first reporter to write of the postwar South. As the southern "territory" was opened to visitors after the war, northern journals began publishing descriptions and commentary on southern places and people. But the earlier reporters had found it newsworthy to picture a rebellious South, casting the black man as hero and his white counterpart as villain. In contrast, a later visitor such as King was much more sympathetic in his portrayal, and the publication of his articles signified a dramatic change in northerners' reporting on the South.[1] Indeed, the shift that King's work represents was not limited to journalism; it affected fiction as well.

In the preface to *The Great South*, an edition of the collected magazine articles, King explained that the purpose of his journey had been to carry out his publishers' desire to

1. Paul H. Buck, *The Road to Reunion, 1865–1900* (Boston: Little, Brown, 1937), 133.

present to their readers a full account of the material resources and the present social and political conditions in the South. In a year and a half, accompanied by several illustrators, King traveled more than twenty-five thousand miles, visiting most major cities and towns in fourteen southern states. He talked with men of every class, party, and color, studied the political developments since Reconstruction in each state, surveyed commercial developments, and explored rivers and mountain regions which, he proudly reported, had been rarely visited by northerners. [2]

King's treatment of the New Orleans area, northern Florida, and North Carolina, all areas that would later be treated at length by other northern visitors, is typical of his work. "Louisiana to-day is Paradise Lost. In twenty years it may be Paradise Regained," he wrote in the opening chapter of *The Great South.* "It has unlimited, magnificent possibilities. Upon its bayou-penetrated soil, on its rich uplands and its vast prairies, a gigantic struggle is in process. It is the battle of race with race, of the picturesque and unjust civilization of the past with the prosaic and leveling civilization of the present" (GS, 17).

He was most impressed with New Orleans' French Quarter and its annual Mardi Gras festivities, exclaiming, "A walk into the French section enchants you; the characteristics of an American city vanish; this might be Toulouse, or Bordeaux, or Marseilles!" (GS, 28). King describes a Mardi Gras ball as "one of the loveliest sights in Christendom. . . . Delicious music swells softly on the perfumed air; the tableaux wax and wane like kaleidoscopic effects, when suddenly the curtain

---

2. Edward King, *The Great South,* ed. W. Magruder Drake and Robert R. Jones (Baton Rouge: Louisiana State University Press, 1972), preface. Hereinafter, references to this work will be cited parenthetically in the text.

rises, and the joyous, grotesque maskers appear upon the ball-room floor" (GS, 44).

King's admiration did not blind him, however, to another aspect of the city—the sad faces of those who had undergone the hardships and humiliation of Reconstruction. He points out hopeful signs, however, such as the growth of the cotton trade and the increased production of sugar, rice, and wheat after the holocaust of war. And he suggests improvements, including a search for minerals that might be profitably mined and sold.

King is highly critical of the legislature placed in Louisiana by the federal government and laments the prevalence of "the rascals and the dubious who get into power" (GS, 97). Because of the lack of knowledge among the black legislators as well as the evil craft of their carpetbagger "advisors," laws had been passed that plunged the state into insurmountable debt and drastically reduced property values. King believes the state's main hope is its educational system, which had grown despite the evils of the political disorganization: "The colored children in the public schools manifest an earnestness and aptitude which amply demonstrates their claim to be admitted to them. People in all sections have ceased grumbling at the 'school-house taxes,' and that in itself is a cheering sign" (GS, 98).

After giving a similar treatment to Texas, Missouri, Tennessee, Arkansas, Mississippi, Alabama, and Georgia, King proceeds to recount his impressions of Florida, stressing the intense natural beauty of the area—the tropical brilliance so much in contrast with the more subdued beauty of northern climates. He spent his first night after entering the state in Jacksonville, near the mouth of the St. Johns River, where he succumbed to rhapsodies on the climate: "This is the South, slumbrous, voluptuous, round and graceful. Here beauty peeps from every door-yard. Mere existence is pleasure; exertion is a bore. Through orange-trees and grand oaks thickly bordering the broad avenues gleams the wide current of the St. John's river" (GS, 380–81). King also reports with exuberance a journey on the Oclawaha River to Silver Springs: "We rowed about on the bosom of this fairy spring, quite overcome with the strangeness of the scene. There is nothing like it elsewhere either in Europe or America; the foliage is even more gorgeously tropical than along the Oclawaha, and its arrangement is more dainty and poetic" (GS, 412).

At all times King's enthusiasm about his surroundings is coupled with a practical eye for their commercial development. He carefully describes the orange crop production, discusses the fertility of the several land areas of the state, and points out the availability of navigable waterways to transport produce. Repeatedly he notes the opportunity for economic progress. In a final section on Florida he presents his impression of the state's political condition: "The Republican party of the State has suffered a good deal at the hands of some of the men who have been intrusted with its interest, so that many citizens of the State who, on national questions, always vote with Republicans, array themselves so far as regards their local interests with the Conservative faction." He advises that "a firm and thoroughly honest administration of State affairs would bring Florida into front rank among the prosperous States in a short time" (GS, 419).

Writing of North Carolina King comments on the "wild carnival of robbery and maladministration" of the first Reconstruction government which had plunged the state into debt and provoked the threat of insurrection in some counties. After the impeachment of Governor Holden, "the white population succeeded in gaining a fair share of influence again." King characteristically ventures a suggestion: "The political troubles may now be considered as nearly over, and if the industrial opportunities of the State are improved, there will be a return to some degree of prosperity" (GS, 469).

King was enthusiastic about the charm and the prospects of Asheville and the French Broad Valley. First noting the potential for mineral mining and the need for a railroad system, he praises the beauty of Asheville: "Beautiful natural parks surround it; superb oaks cast their shadows on greenest of lawns, and noble maples, ash and walnuts border the romantic roadway" (GS, 505). The Indians, he reports, called the French Broad River "'the racing river'" and he finds that "as it hurls its wavelets around the corner of some islet or promontory, one sees how faithfully the name describes the stream. Each separate drop of water seems to be racing with every other" (GS, 507). King also recreates the aura of the mountains for his readers: "As we descended, that afternoon, the pheasant strutted across our path; the cross-bill turned his head archly to look at us; the mountain boomer nervously skipped from tree to tree; the rocks seemed ablaze as we approached the rhododendron thickets; the brooks rippled never so musically, and the azalea's perfume was sweeter than ever before" (GS, 514).

Such was the fare to which the *Scribner's* audience was treated: a mixture of travelogue, local color narrative, and how-to-do-it reform. King had created a successful compound of rapt description, sympathetic social commentary, and potential commercial opportunity. The publishers' hopeful expectations were gratified. The series of articles was so well received that the following year it was republished in book form both in the United States and Great Britain.

To understand why the *Scribner's* publishers initiated the

Great South series and why the South had become such a popular subject at this particular time several questions need to be answered. Were literary and political conditions related to this popularity? What had happened to cause a northern magazine such as *Scribner's* to want to portray the southern states so sympathetically, less than ten years after a bloody war to save the Union? For, throughout the series King's tone was conciliatory—he was hopeful about improvements to be made in the South, and, in contrast to earlier, more self-righteous northern writing, he seemed to deemphasize symptoms of bitterness toward the North after the war.[3] What had brought about this change in attitude on the part of King and other nonsoutherners who visited and wrote about the South?

The war itself was a major factor in creating interest in the South. Both the men who left home to fight and those who waited anxiously for news of them were forced to think about sections outside their native areas, and there was a subsequent growth of curiosity about these other regions. The attention of the nation had been focused on the South, and rather than ending this interest the close of the war brought a number of changes that heightened curiosity.

---

3. Buck in *Road to Reunion*, p. 16, notes that at the close of the war, "the correspondents were now available to enter the heart of the opened territory of the Confederacy and the reading public eagerly awaited their descriptions of the people and the places that had been so prominent in the news of war years. The South itself did nothing... to assist in shaping the publicity so vitally affecting its welfare. The North had only Northerners to do the reporting. And these men possessed in common with their reading public the biased views in regard to the South that had been shaped in time of war." Buck states that the central theme of J. T. Trowbridge's "The South" (1866), which he based on two southern trips, was "that the South was barbarous. The 'spirit of slavery' had debased the Southern mind, destroyed liberty and law, and vitiated all white elements upon which a restored union might be erected" (17–18). Whitelaw Reid's conclusion in *After the War: A Southern Tour*, reports Buck, was that "the Southern people were arrogant and defiant, still nursing the embers of the 'rebellion' and cherishing its ashes" (20). Northerners published much other writing of this tone.

In the prewar period tensions among various sections of the country precluded the acceptance by a northern audience of any sympathetic depiction of the South in fiction. This was also true immediately after the war, when many nonsoutherners still thought of southerners as heathens who must be "democratized" or further punished for their transgressions. In fact, southerners' continued resistance to northern influence only intensified the predominant opinion that the South must be rescued and the way cleared for the implementation of Reconstruction governments.

By the 1870s, however, a very different set of circumstances was in operation. Increasingly, northerners began to question the wisdom of federal intervention in a state's internal affairs. Not only was public opinion shifting in such a way as to facilitate the end of Reconstruction, but new issues were emerging. Pitted against the old idealistic war aims of freeing and protecting the black man were the less idealistic war aims of protecting the interests of the northern commercial establishment.[4] Northern conservatives, threatened by radical labor elements in the East and agrarian radicalism in the West, realized the importance of an alliance with the South. Thus, in 1878, conservative supporters of Republican Rutherford B. Hayes for president, with promises of financial gain for the South, were able to effect a split between northern Democrats, who opposed this kind of aid, and southern Democrats, who felt they needed it.

---

4. C. Vann Woodward, *Origins of the New South, 1877–1913* (Baton Rouge: Louisiana State University Press, 1971), 23, Vol. IX of Wendell Holmes Stephenson and E. Merton Coulter (eds.), *A History of the South* (10 vols.; Baton Rouge: Louisiana State University Press, 1949—). Other helpful works include: Avery Craven, *Reconstruction: The Ending of the Civil War* (New York: Holt, Rinehart, and Winston, 1969); Howard R. Floan, *The South in Northern Eyes, 1831 to 1861* (Austin: University of Texas Press, 1958); and Francis Butler Simkins, *A History of the South* (New York: Alfred A. Knopf, 1963).

When southern Democrats refused to join a filibuster at the Democratic caucus to stop the inauguration of Hayes, Republican papers which had consistently pictured the South as "treasonous, brutal, and disloyal" began to praise that region's good sense and decency.[5] The period following Hayes's election was one of reconciliation, and the South came to be regarded not as a threat to the new economic order but as an important ally. In this new position the carpetbagger kingdom crumbled and the former governing classes of the South regained power. Thus, in the second stage of post-Civil War policy the northern attitude toward the South shifted from one of reform and retribution to that of praise and support. And that change freed writers to seek new approaches in their fictional treatments of the South.

Now that deviation from the national norm was no longer a threat to the Union, depictions in literature of lifestyles free from the taint of northeastern big business and urbanization could be enjoyed for their very differences. And the variety of new and unusual material found in the southern states—the wide range of character types, for example—could easily be incorporated into such fiction. The plantation gentry, the southern poor white, and the black man all appeared exotic to northern readers, the depiction of blacks being especially important. As the crusading zeal of the reformists faded, more and more people began to feel that it was time to let the black man alone and concentrate energies toward new and more pressing problems. The portrayal in fiction of the Negro devoted to his white superiors, deeply religious yet susceptible to superstitious belief, penniless yet happy, and childishly dependent on whites, placated the feelings of the northern read-

5. Woodward, *Origins of the New South,* 43.

ing public and helped dispel any feelings of guilt about leaving the South on its own again.[6]

In addition, an abundance of picturesque detail was available in such southern settings as the ancient cities of St. Augustine and New Orleans, the plantations of the tidewater and Deep South, the rustic mountain villages, and the shanties of the blacks and poor whites. As a journalist, Edward King had merely touched the surface in his descriptive accounts; other writers would fashion this material into greater works.

The South provided the pathos and grandeur of a lost civilization—a defeated country that seemed to urge writers to recount its past before it ultimately disappeared. Of all sections of the country, this one was most in need of preservation through literature before the old order had passed beyond the memory of those who could write about it.[7] And the increasing standardization of speech and lifestyle throughout the country now rendered former differences even more precious. The migration of large numbers of people to northern industrial areas after the war created an audience filled with nostalgia for old times and places, an audience hemmed into cities, looking for entertainment to fill the leisure hours.

The great magazines of the North—*Atlantic Monthly, Harper's, Scribner's*—capitalized on this nostalgia and the de-

6. Louis D. Rubin, Jr., "Introduction to Part III, Southern Writing 1865–1920," in Richard Beale Davis, C. Hugh Holman, and Louis D. Rubin, Jr. (eds.), *Southern Writing, 1585–1920* (New York: Odyssey Press, 1970), 637.

7. Rollin G. Osterweis in *The Myth of the Lost Cause, 1865–1900* (Hamden, Conn.: Shoe String Press, 1973), 32, suggests that newly rich northern businessmen and their wives found the aristocratic tradition attractive because they could now afford to practice it. My own opinion, similar to that of Henry James, is that this newfound wealth usually served as an impediment to truly genteel living. Thus, the aristocratic lifestyle pictured in the South became increasingly elusive to northerners.

mand for quick entertainment. *Scribner's* sent Edward King on
his southern journey, and after witnessing the success of the
Great South series *Harper's* initiated its own southern series by
Edwin De Leon. Other southern sketches appeared in the
seventies.[8] The *Atlantic* followed suit, publishing work by
Mary Murfree and others; by the 1890s, the magazine that
had been regarded as the most hostile to the southern way of
life was jammed with material about it.[9]

Over a twenty-year period, then, nonsouthern writers were
released from their obligations to criticize southern ways and
institutions and became free to praise the South and to
capitalize upon its variety and exoticism. Of course, many of
the attractions readers responded to in the seventies and after
had been present in the South before then, and earlier critical
writers had often struggled unsuccessfully to avoid lapsing into
idealism.

The two trends of criticism and praise are apparent in writings of selected nonsoutherners who visited the South and
wrote about it during and immediately after the Civil War as
well as throughout the Reconstruction period and the decades
following. Harriet Beecher Stowe's work encompasses the entire range from thesis-laden criticism to later blatant praise.
The work of Union soldiers John De Forest and Albion
Tourgée illustrates the thesis-oriented fiction of the war
period, though despite their theses the novels reflect an unconscious idealization of the South. In contrast, the fiction of
Constance Woolson, Lafcadio Hearn, Owen Wister, and
even Henry James reflects the second-stage treatment of the

8. Another excellent example of sympathetic treatment of the South by a northern magazine is the Battles and Leaders of the Civil War series which appeared in
Century Magazine, XXIX–XXXV (1884–87).

9. Buck, *Road to Reunion*, 225. See also Jay B. Hubbell, *The South in American
Literature, 1607–1900* (Durham: Duke University Press, 1954), 726–33.

South—that of rapt praise and overt idealization of the escapist, faraway country. By Wister's time, indeed, the praise even comes to *include* the social thesis. If the novel was an arena for sectional war, as even the supporters and detractors of *Uncle Tom's Cabin* seemed to agree in the 1850s, then so far as northern novelists were concerned the South would seem to have lost the initial battle but won the war.

THE
ENCHANTED
COUNTRY

I

⤙

Harriet Beecher Stowe:
Two Visions of the South

I love to have a day of mere existence. Life itself is a pleasure when the sun shines warm and the lizards dart from all the shingles of the roof and the birds sing in so many notes and tones the yard reverberates—and I sit and dream and am happy and never want to go back north.[1]

The sentiment about the South expressed in this statement is by no means an uncommon one. It becomes ironic only when its author is revealed as the "little lady who wrote the big book that started . . . [the Civil] war," a writer who became famous for pointing out the inequities and horrors of the South's "peculiar institution." But with the conclusion of the Civil War and the resultant removal of political difficulties and the symbol of slavery itself, Harriet Beecher Stowe was no longer bound to a policy of social criticism and was able to enjoy southern voluptuousness. By 1868 she was regularly wintering near Mandarin, Florida, and could enthusiastically recount to her readers and friends the pleasures of southern living.

Palmetto Leaves (1873), less well known than *Uncle Tom's Cabin,* is a collection of letters and descriptive essays, many first published in northern magazines, which chronicles the pleasures of Florida and praises a way of life unlike that of the

---

1. Harriet Beecher Stowe to Annie Fields, 1872, in Edward Wagenknecht, *Harriet Beecher Stowe: The Known and the Unknown* (New York: Oxford University Press, 1965), 81.

urban North. In *Palmetto Leaves* Stowe eulogizes her orange crop as "the veritable golden apples of the Hesperides" and calls the tree itself "the fairest, the noblest, the most generous... the most upspringing and abundant, of all the trees which the Lord God caused to grow eastward in Eden."[2] The joys of picnicking and of sailing on a river which "gently wooes and seduces you" (*PL*, 54) move her to declare that "no dreamland on earth can be more unearthly in its beauty and glory than the St. John's in April" (*PL*, 155). Expanding her praise to encompass all of Florida, Stowe writes, "If we painted her, we should not represent her as a neat, trim dam-sel, with starched linen cuffs and collar: she would be a brunette, dark but comely, with gorgeous tissues, a general disarray and dazzle, and with a sort of jolly untidiness, free, easy, and joyous" (*PL*, 36).

How could Harriet Stowe's attitude have shifted so radi-cally? How could one who had been so hated in the South for her depiction of its wickedness now write in such an idealizing manner? Although the changes in social and political condi-tions are part of the answer, a comparison of northern writers' earlier, critical writing about the South with their later, rap-turous description reveals similarities as well as differences. For in spite of the prescribed social thesis, the stereotyped characters of gentlemen, ladies, and happy slaves, and the praising and idealization of the southern way of life were also present in the earlier works.

Harriet Stowe's concern with the South was a natural out-growth of her family's involvement with the slavery issue. Born in Litchfield, Connecticut, in 1811, Harriet Beecher moved to Cincinnati in 1832 when her father, the Reverend

2. Harriet Beecher Stowe, *Palmetto Leaves* (Boston: James R. Osgood, 1873), 17–18. Hereinafter, references to this work will be cited parenthetically in the text.

Lyman Beecher, founded Lane Theological Seminary. Her marriage four years later to Calvin Stowe, a professor of biblical literature at Lane, kept her in Ohio for eighteen years. As the question of slavery became increasingly a part of church politics, Harriet Stowe, the daughter and wife of ministers, could hardly escape confronting the issue. With the enactment into law of the Fugitive Slave Bill in 1850 obligating nonsoutherners to return fleeing slaves to the South, Stowe, who was now living in Maine where her husband had accepted a position at Bowdoin College, resolved to attack the problem with her pen. Upon receiving a letter from her sister-in-law saying, "Hattie, if I could use a pen as you can, I would write something that will make this whole nation feel what an accursed thing slavery is," she replied, "I will if I live."[3]

Drawing on her experiences with fugitives, such as a slave refugee who became the prototype for Eliza, Stowe began writing what would become *Uncle Tom's Cabin*. She later said that a vision she had in church of the death scene of Uncle Tom formed the story's core. The work was published first in serial form, appearing from June 5, 1851, to April 1, 1852, in the *National Era*. Stowe became consumed with it and when her editors advised her to cut it short and published a note suggesting that her readers might be tiring of the subject, a strong protest resulted.[4]

The publishing history of *Uncle Tom* is sensational. Within a year of its publication in book form on March 20, 1852, 305,000 copies had been sold in America. Another 2,500,000 copies, in English and translation, circulated throughout the world. The southern reaction was also spectacular. In the three years following the appearance of *Uncle Tom's Cabin*, at

3. Edmund Wilson, *Patriotic Gore: Studies in the Literature of the American Civil War*, (Rev. ed.; New York: Oxford University Press, 1966), 31.
4. *Ibid.*, 32.

least fourteen proslavery novels were published as well as numerous pamphlets, articles, and poems. "It was still possible," Edmund Wilson says, "at the beginning of this century for a South Carolina teacher to make his pupils hold up their right hands and swear that they would never read *Uncle Tom.* "[5]

Certainly Stowe's thesis-oriented novel was a departure from the antebellum plantation fiction that had sought to extol and defend southern ways. Yet in leveling her criticisms against slavery and injustice the author employed many of the same devices found in the earlier fiction. For example, a number of black characters in *Uncle Tom* closely approach the stereotype of the happy-go-lucky darkie who is content to be taken care of by the master. The waggish Sam, trusted slave of the Shelbys, impedes the slave trader Haley from catching Eliza and her child, but the author makes clear that Sam's motivation is not his own desire to speed Eliza to freedom (although he certainly wishes her well), but rather his understanding that Mrs. Shelby, his mistress, desires her escape. Therefore Sam capers, rolls his eyeballs, and acts foolish all for the benefit of Mrs. Shelby.

Aunt Chloe, the Shelby's cook, also accepts her place as servant. Explaining to young George Shelby that her position must have been ordained in heaven, she relates to him what she once told her mistress: "Now, Missis, do jist look at dem beautiful white hands o' yourn, with long fingers, and all a sparkling with rings, like my white lilies when the dew's on 'em; and look at my great black stumpin hands. Now, don't ye think de Lord must have meant *me* to make de pie-crust, and you to stay in de parlor?" [6] The slothful Aunt Dinah keeps the

---

5. *Ibid.*, 4.
6. Harriet Beecher Stowe, *Uncle Tom's Cabin* (1852; Garden City, N.Y.: Doubleday, 1960), 39–40. Hereinafter, references to this work will be cited parenthetically in the text.

St. Clare kitchen in a shambles but nevertheless produces some of the finest food in New Orleans. The incorrigible Topsy, if not the stereotype in the novel, soon became one when *Uncle Tom* went on the boards with a singing, dancing imp. Uncle Tom's name, of course, connotes the fawning slave who puts his master's interest above his own.

Thus, for all its antislavery impulse, *Uncle Tom's Cabin* in important ways continues the earlier tradition of romanticizing the South. Stowe's black characters run away only when their condition became truly intolerable. George Harris endures injustice until he sees that he is doomed to be a field hand for life; Eliza flees only to save her son from being sold to Haley. For most blacks, it seems, the idea of freedom is an alien one. And the stereotype of the faithful, childlike slave is evident in the closing pages of the novel when young George Shelby announces to the slaves their freedom: "Many, however, pressed around him, earnestly begging him not to send them away; and, with anxious faces, tendering back their free papers. 'We don't want to be no freer than we are. We's allers had all we wanted. We don't want to leave de ole place, and Mas'r and Missis, and de rest!" (*UTC*, 504–505). Only when George reassures them that they may remain with him on the plantation are they comforted.

Uncle Tom's Cabin shares with the plantation novel of such authors as John Pendleton Kennedy and Thomas Nelson Page a tendency to present southern characters more favorably than their northern counterparts.[7] Miss Ophelia, the aunt of Augustine St. Clare, although certainly a model lady of virtue is a cold stick in comparison with her southern relatives. Her nephew's wife, Marie, a selfish creature whose lack of feeling

7. This has been noted by a number of critics including Joel Chandler Harris and Edmund Wilson.

at times makes her odious to the reader, has a charm that Miss Ophelia lacks. This is apparent in a description of the two women preparing for church: "There she stood, so slender, so elegant, so airy and undulating in all her motions, her lace scarf enveloping her like a mist. She looked a graceful creature, and she felt very good and very elegant indeed. Miss Ophelia stood at her side, a perfect contrast. It was not that she had not as handsome a silk dress and shawl, and as fine a pocket-handkerchief; but stiffness and squareness, and bolt-uprightness, enveloped her with an indefinite yet appreciable a presence as did grace her elegant neighbor" (*UTC*, 213–14). We know that we ought to like Miss Ophelia better, but it's a shame she can't be as pleasing to the eye as Marie.

The archvillain in the novel, of course, is Simon Legree, a northerner whose "fist has got as hard as iron *knocking down niggers*" (*UTC*, 393). Of all characters this New England-born man is the most repulsive—a drunk, a brute, yet superstitious enough to be cowed by a clever mulatto woman. Legree is a crueler slave driver than any southerner in this novel; he is given no redeeming features.

On the whole, southern characters receive the lion's share of favorable qualities.[8] It is Eva, the mistress of slaves, who can civilize Topsy after Miss Ophelia's failure, and Topsy herself understands why Miss Ophelia can't help her: "'She can't bar me, 'cause I'm a nigger!—she'd 's soon have a toad touch her! There can't nobody love niggers, and niggers can't do no-

---

8. Joel Chandler Harris commented that Mrs. Stowe so succumbed to the romance of the plantation "that an anti-slavery tract she was writing—giving it the shape of a novel—is a defense of the system that she intended to attack." Thus, he termed *Uncle Tom's Cabin* "a defense of American slavery as she found it in Kentucky." In Joel Chandler Harris, *Miscellaneous Literary, Political, and Social Writings*, ed. Julia Collier Harris (Chapel Hill: University of North Carolina Press, 1931), 115, 116.

thin'!'" To this Eva responds, "'O Topsy, poor child, *I* love you!'" and places "her little thin, white hand on Topsy's shoulder" *(UTC,* 327–28). Eva can accomplish through simple good feeling what all Miss Ophelia's New England principles are powerless to achieve.

Two white southerners, Augustine St. Clare and the young George Shelby, achieve special status as spokesmen for Stowe's social philosophy. In using southerners as mouthpieces for her ideas, the author employed a device that would be adapted by a number of postbellum writers of reform fiction. She may have felt that a southern character would have more influence on southern readers, but this technique may also reflect the unconscious idealization of the South that seems to permeate *Uncle Tom.*

Augustine St. Clare becomes analogous to "Moore, Byron, Goethe" in his possession of "the gift to appreciate and the sense to feel the finer shades and relations of moral things, [which] often seems an attribute of those whose whole life shows a careless disregard of them." St. Clare is not a religious man, but he is absolved of any guilt—"For, so inconsistent is human nature, especially in the ideal, that not to undertake a thing at all seems better than to undertake and come short" *(UTC,* 354). His shortcomings are explained away in order that we may concentrate on his ideal aspects.

St. Clare is an indulgent master, a long-suffering yet tender husband, and a loving father. Throughout the novel we are reminded of his nobility. When he advises Miss Ophelia that slavery is a business "accursed of God and man.... His fine face, classic as that of a Greek statue, seemed actually to burn with the fervor of his feelings" *(UTC,* 260–61). St. Clare is given the role of prophet as he warns Miss Ophelia of the consequences of slavery in the South and complacency in the North:

"One thing is certain,—that there is a mustering among the masses, the world over; and there is a *dies irae* coming on" (*UTC*, 271).

Unfortunately, St. Clare is killed before he can put into effect his ideas concerning the abolition of slavery. But his role is assumed by young George Shelby, who may be seen as the continuator of St. Clare's ideal position. George, who feels a moral obligation to restore Uncle Tom to the Shelby plantation, undertakes an extensive search for the old slave. He finds him dying on Legree's plantation and vows to address himself to such injustice: "Witness, eternal God... oh, witness, that, from this hour, I will do *what one man can* to drive out this curse of slavery from my land!" (*UTC*, 485). George returns home and within a month gives every slave his freedom papers. St. Clare and George Shelby may be seen, then, as the finest products of a society that, although laboring under the curse of slavery, yet retains a number of qualities the author sees fit to idealize.

For despite its thesis, *Uncle Tom* does idealize the southern way of life—most obviously in Stowe's treatment of the landed gentry, the southern aristocracy. Mrs. Shelby is worshiped by all her servants in her unquestionable position as a lady among ladies. Under her direction the Shelby plantation has every characteristic of grace and goodness. She is a constant reminder to the black servants of their own inferiority, and other lighter colored slaves such as Eliza become refined by emulating her behavior. As a wife, Mrs. Shelby operates as a source of inspiration to her husband, tempering his pragmatism with her gentle ways. Finally, it is in her role as mother that she sends young George on his quest, and through her Christian teaching he is aided in his resolution to free the slaves.

Before dying Uncle Tom states that heaven is better than

Kintuck, but in the context of the novel the two are compara-
ble. Until the arrival of the trader Haley, the Shelby plantation seems the picture of contentment, the slaves thriving and
happy under the loving care of their owners. It is with great
regret that Eliza flees from the home she loves—and Uncle
Tom so loves his master that he is willing to be sold in order to
pay the unavoidable debt. There is never any indication that
other slaves have a desire to leave. Indeed, Shelby plantation
with its vine-covered cottages, pleasant weather, and abundance of Christian fellowship is presented as an ideal spot.

If Shelby plantation is pleasant, St. Clare's home in New
Orleans is a veritable paradise. Except for the demands made
by Marie, here the slaves have little to do but adopt the airs of
their aristocratic master and content themselves with wearing
fine clothes and anticipating the pleasures of the quadroon
ball. Some, like the coal black Aunt Dinah, scorn such emu-
lation of aristocracy and revel in playing the role of complete
mistress of the kitchen quarters, reigning supreme over innu-
merable black children. Although it is clear that this paradise
is a precarious one, dependent entirely upon the presence of
the master, the St. Clare household is for the most part a very
superior place. As Eva puts it, "our way is the pleasantest. . . .
Why, it makes so many more round you to love, you know"
(*UTC*, 218–19).

In contrast, at the Legree "plantation" there are simply
more people round you to hate. The author notes that the
northern-born Simon Legree "governed his plantation by a
sort of resolution of forces. Sambo and Quimbo cordially
hated each other; the plantation hands, one and all, cordially
hated them; and, by playing off one against another, he was
pretty sure, through one or the other of the three parties, to
get informed of whatever was on foot in the place" (*UTC*,
401). It is significant that this setting, different in every re-

spect from the Shelby and St. Clare homes, is the result of the transfer of ownership of a former charming plantation home to the hands of a crass northerner, who but for his geographic locale could almost equally appropriately have been the manager of a textile mill or a steel works. For several pages Stowe laments the decay of a once noble mansion. The smooth lawn and garden are now choked with weeds; the conservatory is a ruin. Only a hint of its past grandeur remains in the form of "a noble avenue of China trees, whose graceful forms and ever-springing foliage seemed to be the only things there that neglect could not daunt or alter,—like noble spirits, so deeply rooted on goodness, as to flourish and grow stronger amid discouragement and decay" (*UTC*, 399–400). Standing in contrast to the simple beauty of the Shelby plantation and the romantic splendor of the St. Clare townhouse, the home of Simon Legree reveals what takes place when one outside of the southern aristocracy takes possession and besmirches the ideal.

Stowe's inconsistencies of attitude become even more apparent in *Dred*, the two volume "sequel" to *Uncle Tom*. [9] Here the author has such difficulty controlling the divergent forces of idealism and criticism that the plot barely holds together. The novel begins as a plantation romance, and the story of the black insurgent Dred, when introduced, actually appears as an intrusion. Stowe was never able to keep the two story lines working together, and only by killing two major characters could she control her plot. Significantly, it is the southern aristocrat Nina and the rebel Dred, representing two counter forces—the Old South and the New—who are eliminated. A

9. Harriet Beecher Stowe, *Dred: A Tale of the Great Dismal Swamp* (2 vols.; Boston: Phillips, Sampson, 1856). Hereinafter, references to this work will be cited parenthetically in the text.

confrontation between the two had to be avoided so that the story could end in a manner palatable to its readers.

In the preface the author explains her choice of a southern setting for *Dred:* "In the near vicinity of modern civilization of the most matter-of-fact kind, exist institutions which carry us back to the twilight of the feudal ages, with all their exciting possibilities of incident" (*D*, I, [iii]). The product of these institutions whom we encounter first is the southern belle, Nina Gordon, who has recently returned to her plantation home after a period of "finishing" at a school in the North and is attempting to choose between several suitors (she is presently engaged to three). Two of them are rather pitiful specimens of northern society, smooth fellows concerned chiefly with appearances. Only the southerner Edward Clayton appears as a likely candidate for a serious romance.

If Nina reflects the stereotype of the languid, light-headed but charming southern girl, Edward is equally representative of the best of southern manhood; he is "ideal to an excess. . . . Ideality pervaded his conscientiousness, urging him always to rise above the commonly-received and so-called practical in morals" (*D*, I, 31). Although he has been admitted to the bar, Edward at the opening of the novel has not taken any cases because the pragmatic aspects of the legal practice are, in his opinion, in conflict with the moral ones.

Edward and Nina are clearly the hero and heroine of the story. As their courtship progresses we are intrigued with the fascination the handsome, high-principled young cavalier has for the careless, sometimes selfish but always charming young girl. The southern setting of their courtship—the plantations of both families—is, as the author stated, a perfect source for romance as we view the couple tête-à-tête on the veranda, riding horseback together, or strolling among the magnolias.

There are, to be sure, some problems in this dreamworld—the appearance of Nina's caddish brother, the inklings of financial troubles for Nina, the frequent references to the sufferings of some of the slaves—but these are muted by Edward's idealism—"There isn't a sublimer power on earth than God has given to us masters" (D, I, 27)—and Nina's complete innocence of the knowledge of suffering. The interest generated for the reader by these two lovers serves to alleviate our concern with the other characters.

The sudden introduction of Dred, black insurrectionist, comes almost as an unwelcome surprise in the midst of the courtship story. Modeling her character to some degree after Nat Turner, the leader of the slave revolt in Southhampton County, Virginia, Stowe describes him as a man "of magnificent stature and proportions. His skin was intensely black, and polished like marble." Dred has "a neck and chest of herculean strength . . . the muscles of a gladiator" (D, I, 240). Inspired, he believes, by the will of God, Dred lives as an outcast in the swamps gathering forces for an insurrection.

Dred is not only a striking example of an independent, proud black man unbent by the belittling effects of slavery; he becomes an almost supernatural figure as the story progresses. Sickened by the hypocritical piety displayed at a camp meeting attended by both races, Dred's voice, coming down from the branches of a tree that hides him, is mistaken for the oracle of God, or at least an angel of wrath: "Hear, O ye rebellious people! The Lord is against this nation! The Lord shall stretch out upon it the line of confusion, and the stones of emptiness!" (D, I, 320). But Dred, presented as a hero and an insurrectionist, creates a problem. We are reassured that his cause is a just one, but Stowe never presumed to go so far as to recommend a black take-over in the South. Consequently, Sterling Brown notes that she has made Dred "less an insurrectionist than a Negro Robin Hood."[10] The only solution is to make a martyr of him, and this is accomplished when he is slain by a band of brutal whites led by Nina's renegade brother, Tom Gordon.

Two forces, then, conflict with each other in the novel. The author continues her moral arguments against slavery, as promoted in *Uncle Tom's Cabin* and embodied in the revolutionary Dred as well as in the antislavery views of Edward Clayton, but through the courtship of Edward and Nina she also idealizes courtly visions of the antebellum South. Another major character, Harry Gordon, is himself a manifestation of this dilemma. For Harry, mulatto half brother to Nina and Tom Gordon, bears the problems of both blacks and whites.[11] Given by his white father all the advantages of an upper-class upbringing, Harry is more a gentleman than is his white brother Tom. Upon the death of Mr. Gordon, Harry is entrusted with the management of the estate and thus is the financial guardian of Nina whom he loves dearly as a sister. Not only is Nina unaware that Harry is her brother; she fails to realize the sacrifices he makes to shield her from the knowledge that there is very little money left in the estate. In fact, Harry has repeatedly spent money saved to purchase his own freedom and that of his wife in order to cover the extravagant expenditures that permit Nina's storybook existence.

Yet Harry Gordon is also a black man; despite his position of responsibility on the plantation he is a slave. Tom Gordon, sensing the superiority of his black half brother, is his sworn enemy, and delights in threatening to take Harry's wife as a

10. Sterling Brown, *The Negro in American Fiction* (Albany: J. B. Lyon Press, 1937), 39.

11. For an excellent discussion of Harry Gordon see the chapter entitled "Harry Gordon's Dilemma" in Alice C. Crozier's, *The Novels of Harriet Beecher Stowe* (New York: Oxford University Press, 1969).

mistress. And Harry is faced with another force—the accusations made by Dred that he is a traitor to the black race in
using his education and position of authority not for his fellow
blacks, but for the benefit of Nina Gordon.

As Harry agonizes over his role, so too does the author.
Should Harry devote himself to maintaining Nina's idealized
existence—or should he heed Dred's urgings to give allegiance
to his black brothers? Harry fails to initiate action and only
after Stowe removes Nina from the story by means of a fatal
illness (an action that entirely violates the continuity of the
romance plot) does he follow Dred. Even then Dred is killed,
thus freeing Harry from the burden of his choice. At the
conclusion of the novel Harry and his wife escape to Canada,
certainly a justifiable choice, but one which was an easy alternative for Stowe.

If Harry Gordon fails to act until acted upon, so does the
author, and for this reason *Dred,* lacking a central controlling
force, fails to hold together. Instead the Nina-Edward romance is cut off awkwardly, and the story of Dred also remains
unresolved. As in *Uncle Tom's Cabin,* the author struggles to
reconcile moral precepts with rampant idealization, but in
Dred these idealized aspects bring the story to an impasse.

Still, although the only resolution Stowe offered to the
problems in the South was escape to Canada, she did provide
her audience with a good bit of pleasant entertainment—
entertainment, however, based upon and perpetuating the
traditional, stereotyped ways of looking at the South and even
evoking the ideals with which the author was ostensibly doing
battle. A case in point is the slave Tiff. When his young
mistress makes an unfortunate marriage with a man of poor
white extraction, he follows her into exile, provides her with a
living, and becomes nurse to her children. Upon the death of
his mistress, Tiff becomes sole benefactor and protector for the

young orphans. Now all of this is noble indeed, but Stowe further characterizes Tiff as a caricature of the fawning, groveling Negro. Tiff, certain that he is more than a "poor white folks' nigger," worships Nina Gordon who represents to him the highest form of ladyhood. In addition to keeping his two charges from starving, he desires to bring them up as a real lady and gentleman. He instructs the young girl, "Miss Fanny," to emulate Nina, tells the children "young ladies and gen'lemen must n't talk like niggers," and at the camp meeting at which Dred makes his appearance Tiff instructs the children to "order me round *well* . . . 'cause what's de use of having a nigger, and nobody knowing it?" (D, I, 278, 289).

In another episode Tiff politely turns down Nina's offer of her servant Milly to instruct the children in the Bible. He asks Nina to read to his charges, explaining that he prefers "white teaching" and implying that of course he wants the children to be saved, but he also wishes them to be *cultivated.* To Tiff, the old way of aristocracy founded on slavery is the only way. With this character the author, even though unintentionally, makes the idea seem not only palatable but admirable.

Other examples of blacks who illustrate the old stereotypes for the reader's amusement include Tomtit, an impudent young scalawag who repeatedly provides such entertainment as that at the camp meeting attended by the Gordon slaves. The setting is the Gordon tent in which a group is undergoing a religious experience:

A circle of men and women, interspersed with children, were sitting, with their eyes shut, and their heads thrown back, singing at the top of their voices. Occasionally, one or other would vary the exercises by clapping of hands, jumping up straight into the air, falling flat on the ground, screaming, dancing, and laughing.
    "O, set me up on a rock!" screamed one.
    "I's sot up!" screamed another.

"Glory!" cried the third, and a tempest of "amens" poured in between.

"I's got a sperience!" cried one, and forthwith began piping it out in a high key, while others kept on singing.

"I's got a sperience!" shouted Tomtit, whom Aunt Rose, with maternal care, had taken with her.

"No, you an't, neither! Sit down!" said Aunt Rose, kneading him down as if he had been a batch of biscuits, and going on at the same time with her hymn.

"I's on the Rock of Ages!" screamed a neighbor.

"I want to get on a rock edgeways!" screamed Tomtit, struggling desperately with Aunt Rose's great fat hands.

"Mind yourself!—I'll crack you over!" said Aunt Rose. And Tomtit, still continuing rebellious, *was* cracked over accordingly, with such force as to send him head-foremost on the straw at the bottom of the tent (*D*, I, 297–98).

For all the author's stated desire to promote in her fiction sympathy for the plight of the enslaved black man, a character such as Tomtit is no more than the amusing pickaninny who appeared in similar form in the earlier plantation novels. It seems that despite her intentions the author is bedazzled with Nina Gordon and her fellow aristocrats. After making critical remarks about people going to religious gatherings out of curiosity rather than to pray, she proceeds to entertain us with the antics of Tomtit and then to inform us that our laughter is shared by Nina Gordon, who is also a spectator to the scene.

Tomtit and Tiff are only symptomatic of the haze of idealism obscuring *Dred*. Stowe's fascination with southern life is evidenced repeatedly in the book, as in her description of Edward Clayton's sister Anne and Magnolia Grove, her plantation: "Anne Clayton, in a fresh white morning-wrapper, with her pure, healthy complexion, fine teeth, and frank, beaming smile, looked like a queenly damask rose. A queen she really was on her own plantation, reigning by the

strongest of all powers, that of love" (*D,* II, 46). Stowe comments that Anne's beauty and grace are worshiped by her
slaves: "The negro race, with many of the faults of children,
unite many of their most amiable qualities, in the simplicity
and confidingness with which they yield themselves up in
admiration of a superior friend" (*D,* II, 46). Although Anne is
a reformer who wishes to educate her slaves, the author dwells
upon her qualities as a lady. And the admiration shown by the
slaves is akin to the idealism pervading the book. If *Dred* ends
nowhere but in the death of Nina and Dred and the removal
of the other major characters to Canada, it is probably because
the author's conflicting attitudes could not bring her to any
firmer resolution.

The point is that even though Stowe's writing immediately
preceding and during the Civil War was in certain ways hostile to the South, there remained constant a degree of idealization of the region as the proverbial faraway country where life
might be lived in a leisurely, even courtly, fashion impossible
in the modern North. Works such as *Uncle Tom's Cabin* and
Dred thus contain the seeds of attitudes that would come into
full flower in the later writing.

Palmetto Leaves can be understood, then, as a continuation
of this idealizing process. Stowe's initial interest in Florida was
the result of philanthropic and maternal concerns. She rented
a cotton plantation, Laurel Grove, in the spring of 1867,
hoping to provide her son, Frederick, who had been wounded
in the war, with a project and a place of recuperation and, at
the same time, wanting to give employment to black laborers.[12] Although Stowe lost ten thousand dollars in this experiment and neither her son nor the former slaves were ben-

12. Mary B. Graff, *Mandarin on the St. Johns* (Gainesville: University of Florida
Press, 1953), 44.

efited, her Florida visit convinced her that this place would make an ideal residence.[13] She purchased thirty acres with orange groves, expanded a hut on the property into a cottage, and between 1868 and 1884 the Stowe family regularly wintered in Mandarin.

During these winters Stowe occasionally occupied herself writing travel articles and letters describing her surroundings. These works were among the earliest promotional writings for Florida, and in this unsolicited testimony she pictured the state as a tropical paradise.[14] Stowe's Florida writings began appearing soon after her arrival in sketches she wrote weekly for *Hearth and Home*.[15] She began writing for the *Christian Union* in 1870, and in 1872 she continued in Florida a literary project she hoped would keep her works regularly published in the *Christian Union* and would result in the book-length work she had promised James R. Osgood. She had promised Osgood a novel, but she contributed an "occasional Palmetto leaf" to the *Christian Union,* and in 1873 Osgood brought out *Palmetto Leaves,* a collection of most of these articles.[16]

Although *Palmetto Leaves* is nonfiction, it resembles the popular local color fiction of the time in its elaborate attention to details of setting. Significantly, in this work the author abandoned any attempt to promote the strong thesis of reform that appears in her earlier writings. A sense of complacency pervades the discussions of flowers and orange groves, picnics and river tours. The author states that a primary purpose in coming to Florida was that of founding a colony with a church

13. *Ibid.*

14. Forrest Wilson, *Crusader in Crinoline: The Life of Harriet Beecher Stowe* (Philadelphia: J. B. Lippincott, 1941), 576.

15. John R. Adams, *Harriet Beecher Stowe* (New York: Twayne Publishers, 1963), 116.

16. Wilson, *Crusader in Crinoline,* 576.

and schoolhouse under the auspices of the Freedman's Bureau, yet very little is said about this project. The two buildings are destroyed by a fire, and after a brief lament and assurances to her readers that the fire was probably the result of carelessness and not of malice, the author resumes her cataloguing of the splendors of Florida.

The stereotyped character appearing in *Palmetto Leaves* is characteristic of local color writing. Stowe presents few individuals, describing old black Cudjo, for example, as "black as night itself; and but for a glittering, intellectual eye, he might have been taken for a big baboon,—the missing link of Darwin" (*PL,* 269). She notes that many blacks are living outside the legal bond of marriage, but rather than urging reform she turns the subject into humorous anecdote: "But the men seemed to regard this [marriage] as the imposing of a yoke beyond what they could bear. Mose said he had one wife in Virginny, and one in Carliny; and how did he know which of 'em he should like best? Mandy, on the female side, objected that she could not be married yet for want of a white lace veil, which she seemed to consider essential to the ceremony. The survey of Mandy in her stuff gown and cow-hide boots, with her man's hat on, following the mule with the plough, brought rather ludicrous emotions in connection with this want of a white veil" (*PL,* 291).

In the closing chapter of *Palmetto Leaves,* entitled "The Laborers of the South," Stowe gives southerners some practical advice—advice very unlike the accusations of exploitation she leveled against white southerners in her earlier works. In answer to the question raised in Florida of "Who shall work for us?" she replies that "the negro is the natural laborer of tropical regions. He is immensely strong; he thrives and flourishes physically under a temperature that exposes a white man to disease and death." She cites as evidence a captain employed in a Government Coast Survey who fitted his ship with blacks when undertaking a voyage involving "much hard labor, exposure to the fiercest extremes of tropical temperature, and sojourning and travelling in swamps and lagoons, often most deadly to the white race." The venture was a complete success and despite the hardships "the gayety and good nature which belonged to the race made their toils seem to sit lighter upon them than upon a given number of white men" (*PL*, 283–84).

Both *Uncle Tom's Cabin* and *Dred* urge education for Negroes. In *Palmetto Leaves* this is reiterated, but the emphasis is different: "All that is wanted to supply the South with a set of the most desirable skilled laborers is simply education. The negro children are bright; they can be taught anything: and if the whites, who cannot bear tropical suns and fierce extremes, neglect to educate a docile race who both can and will bear it for them, they throw away their best chance of success in a most foolish manner" (*PL*, 317). The author's concluding statement sounds surprisingly reminiscent of antebellum southern sentiment: "Those who understand and know how to treat the negroes seldom have reason to complain of their ingratitude" (*PL*, 285). But discussion of the economics of black labor occupies only a small place in *Palmetto Leaves*. Stowe's primary interest is to present Florida as a veritable southern Eden.[17] She has come not to blame but to praise, and if a little practical advice is necessary from time to time, it is not intended to detract from the larger picture.

Stowe's writings, spanning a thirty-year period before and after the war, thus encompass the transition in the treatment

17. In John R. Adams (ed.), *Harriet Beecher Stowe, Regional Sketches: New England and Florida* (New Haven: College and University Press, 1972), Adams in his introduction notes that Stowe had planned to write a novel about Florida to be entitled *Orange Blossoms*. There is no evidence that she ever began the project.

of the South in fiction from thesis-oriented novels ostensibly criticizing southern institutions and morals to later works overtly praising the region. But the distance from Shelby plantation to Mandarin, Florida, was clearly not as great as it might have seemed.

II

Northern Reformers and the Southern Mystique: The Fiction of John De Forest and Albion Tourgée

One might suppose that with the ending of the Civil War, weary Union soldiers, hoping to reconstruct a normal world for themselves in the North, would have happily turned their backs on the war-torn South. On the contrary, a number returned to the South, serving in the newly established military governments or performing duties in Reconstruction machinery such as the Freedman's Bureau. In contrast to what was possible for soldiers in wartime, participants in these programs were able to observe their southern surroundings in greater depth and at a more leisurely pace.

John W. De Forest and Albion Tourgée were two such observers who wrote novels promoting political and social reform in the South shortly after the Civil War.[1] Both were northerners who had participated in the war—De Forest as a captain, Tourgée as a lieutenant. De Forest returned to serve for eighteen months as agent in the Freedman's Bureau in Greenville, South Carolina; Tourgée was a Reconstruction judge in Greensboro, North Carolina, for a number of years.

1. A recent treatment of De Forest and Tourgée is Daniel Aaron's *The Unwritten War: American Writers and the Civil War* (New York: Alfred A. Knopf, 1973). Most of *American Literary Realism*, I (Fall, 1968), is devoted to John De Forest and includes a critical bibliography as well as articles dealing with various aspects of his work. See *American Literary Realism*, VIII (1975), 53–80, for an annotated bibliography of Tourgée including a history of criticism, discussion of editions and reprints, description of manuscript collections, and biography.

Tourgée's commitment to a life in the South was much greater than that of De Forest. He invested his savings in his southern property, attempted to bring about reforms, and stayed for many years, whereas De Forest limited himself to performing only those duties prescribed by the Freedman's Bureau and after a brief period of service returned to the North, living most of his life in New Haven. Despite these differences, the two men shared a common concern: in writing novels that implicitly and explicitly compared southern society with that of the North, both commented on the inadequacies of the southern system and made suggestions for reform.

1.

The youngest of four sons of a prosperous family, John De Forest was born in Seymour, Connecticut, in 1826, educated in private schools, and as a youth spent time in the Near East with a brother in hopes of improving his poor health. He had literary aspirations early in life. In 1851 he published *The History of the Indians of Connecticut,* and other works soon followed, including two travel books, *Oriental Acquaintance* (1856) and *European Acquaintance* (1858), as well as short stories and two novels.[2]

Introverted and frail during his youth, De Forest gave little indication that he would become a good soldier and the author of a successful war novel. When he began recruiting a company for the Twelfth Connecticut Volunteers in the fall of 1861, he was already thirty-five, married, and a father. Of a conservative bent, he appeared cool and a little priggish.[3] His experiences in the field, however, rapidly transformed him from dilettante to capable soldier. Between January, 1862,

2. E. R. Hagemann, "A Checklist of the Writings of John William De Forest (1826–1906)," in *Studies in Bibliography,* VIII (1956), 185–94.
3. Aaron, *The Unwritten War,* 165.

and December, 1864, he served as a field officer in Louisiana and Virginia. As he noted in the preface to a volume of verse, "I was on three storming parties, six days of field engagement, and thirty-seven days of siege duty, making forty-six days under fire."[4] During this period he readjusted his romantic conception of war, finding that "bayonet fighting occurs mainly in newspapers and other works of fiction."[5]

Upon leaving the army, De Forest was nominated early in 1865 for a captaincy in the Veteran Reserve Corps and served for a time in Washington, D.C. From October, 1866, until January, 1868, he was acting assistant commissioner in the Freedman's Bureau subdistrict in Greenville, South Carolina.[6] Here, in what he termed his satrapy, he encountered the various classes of southerners whom he classified and later wrote about as "the new man and brother (the Negro), the low-down people (the poor white trash), the semi-chivalrous Southrons (the small farmers of the mountains who remained Union supporters during the war), and the chivalrous Southrons (the plantation aristocrats)."[7]

De Forest's accounts of his experiences in the army and as an agent in the Freedman's Bureau appear in two volumes: *A Volunteer's Adventures* and *A Union Officer in the Reconstruction*.[8] His blend of realism and irony in describing the heroics

4. John W. De Forest, *Poems: Medley and Palestrina* (New Haven: Tuttle, Morehouse, and Taylor, 1902), ix.
5. John William De Forest, *A Volunteer's Adventures: A Union Captain's Record of the Civil War*, ed. James H. Croushore (New Haven: Yale University Press, 1946), 66.
6. Hagemann, "Checklist," 185–86.
7. James F. Light, *John William De Forest* (New Haven: College and University Press, 1965), 81.
8. For an account of the compilation of *A Volunteer's Adventures* see the preface to the 1946 edition edited by James Croushore. Between 1868 and 1869 De Forest published nine Reconstruction articles which later in his life he put together as a second volume in his projected two volume *Military Life*. In 1948 Croushore and David Potter edited and published it as *A Union Officer in the Reconstruction* (New Haven: Yale University Press, 1948).

and foolery of war is apparent, as in an account of the orders of an inexperienced lieutenant colonel who sent him "across the bayou on a railroad bridge to occupy an isolated house and hold it against the alligators, who bellowed around us all night like bulls of Bashan. The position was perfectly ridiculous, and, if the enemy had appeared, it would have been disastrous." Cynically, De Forest concluded, "It is part of a man's business in the army to obey and respect his inferiors."[9]

De Forest was a prolific fiction writer as well and wrote short stories and several novels based on southern material. His best-known work, *Miss Ravenel's Conversion from Secession to Loyalty* (1867), appeared shortly after he left active military duty and is modeled on many of his personal war experiences. *Kate Beaumont* (1872) is set in the Pickens district in which De Forest served as an agent in the Freedman's Bureau. After writing a number of novels dealing with politics and corruption in Washington, De Forest, late in his life, drew again on a southern theme for *The Bloody Chasm* (1881), which was virtually ignored by readers and critics alike.[10] Written according to the tenets of romanticism rather than realism, this novel fails to attain the quality of the earlier novels about the South.

De Forest played an important role in the development of American literary realism.[11] His unflinching account not only

9. De Forest, *A Volunteer's Adventures,* 81–82.

10. De Forest wrote numerous short stories, some of which, such as "Rum Creeters is Women," *Harper's,* XXXIV (March, 1867), 484–91, employ a formula—reconciliation through romance—which might be termed a model for a later flood of postwar fiction in which a North-South romance became a vehicle for promoting sectional reconciliation. See Light's *John W. De Forest* for an extensive discussion of the short stories and p. 163 for a discussion of *The Bloody Chasm.*

11. See Gordon S. Haight, "Realism Defined: William Dean Howells," *Literary History of the United States: History,* ed. Robert E. Spiller *et al.* (Rev. ed., New York: Macmillan, 1963), 881. Haight refers to De Forest as "the first American writer to deserve the name of realist."

of the bravery of the front lines but also of the cowardliness of deserters and the brutality and suffering endured by soldiers was unique in the fiction of the time. A good case has been made that his realistic accounts of battle scenes may have influenced Crane's *The Red Badge of Courage.* [12]

De Forest's view of the novel as an instrument for reform is apparent in his unsigned article appearing in the *Nation*, January, 1868, entitled, "The Great American Novel." In attempting to explain the absence of a "great American Novel" he clarified the purposes of his own fiction, particularly his recently published novel, *Miss Ravenel's Conversion*. Briefly surveying American literary productions of the past and present, including the works of Washington Irving, James Fenimore Cooper, Nathaniel Hawthorne, and Oliver Wendell Holmes, as well as lesser figures such as James Paulding, Charles Brown, John Pendleton Kennedy, and William Gilmore Simms, De Forest concludes that, despite valiant attempts, none of these succeeds in fulfilling the requisites of the "Great Novel." Interestingly, there is one writer who, in De Forest's opinion, approaches the standard of greatness. "The nearest approach to the desired phenomenon is 'Uncle Tom's Cabin,'" he contends, though he readily concedes its imperfections. "There were very noticeable faults in that story; there was a very faulty plot; there was (if idealism be a fault) a black man painted whiter than the angels, and a girl such as girls are to be, perhaps, but are not yet." But these faults are far outweighed by the novel's virtues: "There was... a national breadth to the picture, truthful outlining of character, natural speaking, and plenty of strong feeling. Though comeliness of form was lacking, the material of the work was in many re-

---

12. Thomas F. O'Donnell, "De Forest, Van Petten, and Stephen Crane," *American Literature*, XXVII (January, 1956), 578–79.

spects admirable." De Forest concludes: "Such Northerners as Mrs. Stowe painted we have seen; and we have seen such Southerners, no matter what the people south of Mason and Dixon's line may protest; we have seen such negroes, barring, of course, the impeccable Uncle Tom—uncle of no extant nephews, so far as we know. It was a picture of American life, drawn with a few strong and passionate strokes, not filled in thoroughly, but still a portrait."[13]

De Forest's comments on Stowe's writing might well be applied to some of his own work. Throughout *Miss Ravenel's Conversion,* he adopts the same attitude as Stowe toward northern and southern society. And although his portrayal of northern society includes a number of frivolous and pathetic characters, the hero is the personification of the three Yankee virtues of temperance, steadfastness, and high moral standards. De Forest does not attempt to create an Uncle Tom—he settles for a devout black preacher hampered by a roving eye for women. His evaluation of *Uncle Tom's Cabin,* however, indicates that he found Stowe's "novel as moral" agreeable to his own writing purposes.

Miss Ravenel's Conversion received more critical acclaim than did many of his later works. Although it did not sell well at the time of its publication in 1867 to a public grown weary of reading of war, it is probably, as Howells says, one of the best works of fiction in terms of its realism to come out immediately after the Civil War. De Forest used the war as the backdrop for his tale of the love affair between a southern belle and a Yankee soldier: "It was shortly after the capitulation of loyal Fort Sumter to rebellious South Carolina that Mr. Edward Colburne of New Boston made the acquaintance

13. John William De Forest, "The Great American Novel," *Nation,* VI (January 9, 1868), 28.

of Miss Lillie Ravenel of New Orleans." [14] As the novel opens Miss Ravenel has already been transplanted to New Boston from her beloved South. She finds the town a rather stuffy and prim place where, as Colburne half-jestingly remarks, "We are so temperate that we are disposed to outlaw the raising of rye." Although the times are becoming more liberal, he adds, "There used to be such a solemn set of Professors [at the university] that they couldn't be recognized in the cemetery because they had so much the air of tombstones" (MRC, 41–42).

In spite of New Boston's many shortcomings, however, the people there are honorable. When Lillie returns to New Orleans with her father, she views her southern acquaintances with new eyes and is shocked to find how inferior they are to her northern friends. Witnessing some New Orleans women discussing political affairs "metaphorically tying Beast Butler to a flaming stake and performing a scalp dance around it, making a drinking cup of his skull, quaffing from it refreshing draughts of Yankee blood," Lillie recollects that "disagreeably loyal as the New Boston ladies were, she had not heard from their lips any such conversational atrocities" (MRC, 145).

When a New Orleans native, under cover of dark, clubs Dr. Ravenel, he comments wryly, "It's only an ordinary New Orleans salutation. I knew I was in New Orleans when I was hit, just as the shipwrecked man knew he was in a Christian country when he saw a gallows." He allows that in this city, "It is one of our pretty ways to brain people by surprise" (MRC, 156). Lillie and the reader must concede that although things may be stodgy in New Boston, this is preferable to maliciousness and violence.

14. John William De Forest, *Miss Ravenel's Conversion from Secession to Loyalty* (Columbus, Ohio: Charles E. Merrill, 1969), [7]. Hereinafter, references to this work will be cited parenthetically in the text.

The story line itself—the conversion of Miss Ravenel—most clearly illustrates the author's convictions. In the opening pages of the novel Lillie is presented as a steadfast rebel: "I admit that Louisiana is not perfect. But it is my Louisiana. . . . I think we owe fealty to our State, and should go with it wherever it goes" (MRC, 18). However, after witnessing the atrocities of war (largely committed by southerners in this novel) and being won by the valiant Colburne, Lillie's opinions change. When her father states that "but for these Yankees and their cold moral purity, we should have established a society on the basis of the most horrible slavery that the world has known since the days of pagan Rome," Lillie accords "acquiescence and sympathy; her conversion from secession and slavery was complete" (MRC, 507).

Lillie's suitor, Captain Colburne, represents the finest New Boston, and the North, can offer. An introductory description pictures a young man "sympathetic, earnest in his feelings, as frank as such a modest fellow could be" (MRC, 25). In battle he is brave and a good leader, as an officer he is conscientious and self-sacrificing. When Dr. Ravenel and Lillie attempt to run a plantation manned by freedmen, it is Colburne who saves them from a rebel attack. And when Lillie marries Colonel Carter (a Virginian in the Union army) and virtually forgets Colburne's existence, he remains faithful to her. Probably the only disagreeable trait the author relinquishes to Colburne is that of allowing him to feel inferior to his charming leader, Carter.

Although Colonel Carter's credentials at first appear quite impressive, in introducing him the author leaves us somewhat in doubt: "There was a cavalier dash in the gentleman's tone and manner; he looked and spoke as if he felt himself quite good enough for his company. And so he was, at least in respect to descent and social position." The reader immediately begins to wonder what his qualities are in other respects. Carter is a graduate of West Point, a former officer in the regular service, and a lieutenant colonel in the Second Barataria "which was shortly to distinguish itself by a masterly retreat from Bull Run" (MRC, 29). In contrast to Colburne's temperance and faithfulness, Carter pursues numerous debauches even after his marriage to Lillie. To his credit, however, he acts a gentleman to his wife and her father, and his final financial ruin results from his illegal attempts to support his wife in a splendid manner. Carter cannot be viewed as a singularly evil man so much as an intemperate one—a person who because of a rather lax upbringing and weak morals is not good enough for our heroine.

Colonel Carter is a rather mild form of southern evil, however, compared to Lillie's deceitful cousin, Mrs. Larue. Howells in his review of the novel recoiled from her: "There is a little too much of her,—it is as if the wily enchantress had cast her glamour upon the author himself,—and there is too much anxiety that the nature of her intrigue with Carter shall not be misunderstood."[15] Howells was disgusted with Mrs. Larue's vulgarity; he did not note that De Forest chose to cast a southern lady in this role. Although the maidens of New Boston are flighty and light-headed, they are not capable of Mrs. Larue's two-faced loyalties—to either the Union or the Confederacy, depending on which will serve her purposes best at a particular moment—and her deliberate, calculated seduction of Colonel Carter after his marriage to Lillie.

De Forest's most persuasive and outspoken character for reform is Lillie's father, Dr. Ravenel. It is through this man, a native of the South who is enlightened enough to be emanci-

---

15. William Dean Howells, review of *Miss Ravenel's Conversion from Secession to Loyalty, Atlantic Monthly*, XX (July, 1867), 122.

pated from its shortcomings, that the author makes some of his most telling statements. The doctor comments that Confederate soldiers "have been educated under an awful tyranny of prejudice, conceit, and ignorance. They are more incapable of perceiving their own true interests than so many brutes. I have had the honor to be acquainted with dogs who were their superiors in that respect" (MRC, 343–44). On the war, he says, "The Inquisition, the Massacre of St. Bartholomew, were common sense and evangelical mercy compared to this pro-slavery rebellion. And yet these imps of atrocity pretend to be Christians." Adding that he would not be surprised if they prayed to God for the continuance of slavery, he concludes, "But God would not wait for them to reach this acme of iniquity. His patience is exhausted, and He is even now bringing them to punishment" (MRC, 309–10).

Dr. Ravenel puts into words the theme of the novel: "The pro-slavery South meant oligarchy, and imitated the manners of the European nobility. The democratic North means equality—every man standing on his own legs, and not bestriding other men's shoulders" (MRC, 506). He acknowledges that the North had, in effect, saved the South from the dreadful blunder of promulgating slavery. Although the novel ends shortly after the war, there is enough groundwork laid to establish prerogatives for continued northern efforts to remedy and improve conditions in the South.

In 1872 De Forest published *Kate Beaumont*, a novel treating prewar southern society. Significantly, the hero is a southerner, Frank McAlister, who has spent a number of years in Europe pursuing education and travel. Returning to his native South Carolina, he is appalled at the barbaric institutions of his homeland. As one character in the novel, Major Lawson, states several times, this is a Romeo and Juliet story in the South. Frank McAlister meets and falls in love with Kate

Beaumont on his return voyage from Europe. Unfortunately, the low country Beaumonts and the highland McAlisters have been feuding for a number of years and, being representative of southern gentility, are experts at interpreting and living by the southern code of honor. In adhering to the institutions of the code duello, however, they are victims of foolish pride. Frank and Kate suffer the full impact of the family feud, and only after a number of near duels, family quarrels, and compromises, are the lovers able to marry.

In this picture of South Carolina life De Forest seems to be suggesting that although such a society may preserve the old world charms of courtliness and a sense of honor, its main effect, unfortunately, is to debilitate its inhabitants and reduce their lives to an endless round of petty insults and quarrels. Again, the point seems clear; the South would do well to look to the northern section of the nation for guidance and to profit by its example.

2.

As a literary figure, Albion Winegar Tourgée is of considerably less stature than De Forest. His place in the development of American literary realism is slight, and the interest in his work today stems chiefly from the historicity of his portrayal of life in the Reconstruction South. Like De Forest, Tourgée's service in the Union army provided him with his first experience of any length in the South.

Born in Ashtabula County, Ohio, in 1838, Tourgée was influenced as a child by his strict Methodist father. The deep religious awareness and a liking for debate which were instilled in him by the elder Tourgée became motivating factors in the son's judicial career and in his writing.[16] Tourgée entered the

---

16. Theodore Gross, *Albion W. Tourgée* (New Haven: College and University Press, 1963), 17. This work is convenient for quick reference to major biographical

Kingsville Academy in Kingsville, Ohio, in 1854, and upon his graduation in 1859 he enrolled in the University of Rochester. Letters written during this time indicate that he had little use for politics while at the university, but by the latter part of 1860 his interest in national affairs had increased, as is indicated by his being elected captain of the "Rochester Wide Awake Club," a group supporting the Republican cause.[17] In January of 1861, Tourgée left the university because of financial problems and in April enlisted with the 27th New York Volunteers. Taking part in the first battle of Bull Run, July 4, 1861, he was wounded in the spine. After receiving an honorable discharge, he returned to Ashtabula where he began studying law.

Although his spine injury continued to plague him, Tourgée felt compelled by July, 1862, to return to the army. Commissioned first lieutenant in Company G of the 105th Ohio Volunteers, he remained with this company until his discharge January 1, 1864. During this period he participated in or witnessed the battles of Chickamauga, Chattanooga, Lookout Mountain, and Missionary Ridge.[18]

Within a year, the recently discharged soldier had decided to make his future in the South. In 1865 he bought property and with his family moved to Greensboro, North Carolina. Tourgée's attitudes did little to endear him to his southern neighbors; he began immediately to espouse his beliefs that the South must be "Americanized" and the black man raised to an equal status with whites.[19]

This period of southern residence, lasting from 1865 until

facts and for brief but perceptive analyses of many of Tourgée's works. For a more comprehensive treatment of Tourgée's life see Otto H. Olsen, *Carpetbagger's Crusade: The Life of Albion Winegar Tourgée* (Baltimore: Johns Hopkins Press, 1965).

17. Gross, *Albion W. Tourgée*, 18.
18. *Ibid.*, 19.
19. *Ibid.*

1879, is of greatest interest in an analysis of Tourgée as representative Reconstruction writer. He served as delegate to the
Loyalist convention in Philadelphia in 1866, became the
editor of a Republican newspaper, The Union Register, which
in 1867 failed, played an active role in the North Carolina
Reconstruction Convention of 1868, and in March of 1868
became a judge of the Superior Court, Seventh Judicial District of North Carolina. By 1876, Tourgée had alienated
enough of his southern neighbors to make life unbearable in
Greensboro, and he accepted an appointment as pension
agent in Raleigh. In September, 1879, he left North Carolina,
never again to live in the South, although he drew on his
southern experiences for many more years in his writing.

Tourgée's role as a writer of Reconstruction literature was
unique. He was the only northerner who lived in the South
for the duration of the period, served as an active politician in
the regime, and wrote extensively about it.[20] Like De Forest
he wrote both fictional and nonfictional accounts of his southern experiences. Most of his many articles for newspaper and
journal publication were attempts to persuade southerners of
the need to make changes and to warn northerners not to
neglect their duties in reforming the South. His literary reputation, however, rests upon his novels, of which he wrote
more than a dozen, approximately half dealing with the
South. He was best when functioning as a reporter and at a
loss when attempting to construct a calculated plot and original story. Thus the quality of these novels varies greatly, with
A Fool's Errand and Bricks Without Straw being the best of the
Reconstruction works.[21] In these novels Tourgée's interpreta-

20. Theodore Gross, "Albion W. Tourgée: Reporter of the Reconstruction,"
Mississippi Quarterly, XVI (Summer, 1963), 111.
21. Tourgée began writing Toinette while living in North Carolina and published
it under a pseudonym in 1874; it was renamed A Royal Gentleman in 1881. In Albion

tion of the problems of Reconstruction, based on his own experiences, is apparent, giving them an historical validity lacking in many of his other works.[22]

Tourgée was well aware of the wealth of material the South had to offer the fiction writer, and he consciously used it to create not only entertaining stories but also persuasive tracts intended to prick the conscience of his northern readers and convince them of the necessity of continued support for the black man in the South and for the recently established governments.[23] Both A *Fool's Errand* and *Bricks Without Straw* are problem novels in the sense that they leave the reader feeling that more must be done to rectify the wrongs presented. Although Tourgée implied that he was only concerned with recording his surroundings, it is evident that his presentation of the South is concerned less with description for its own sake than with reform.

In a letter to the publishers which forms a preface to an edition of A *Fool's Errand,* Tourgée defined the fool: "He differs from his fellow-mortals chiefly in this, that he sees or

---

W. *Tourgée* Gross notes that "it set the oft-repeated pattern for his later novels; it was the first work of fiction to deal directly with the problem of Reconstruction; and its sentimental description of the conflict between the Southern aristocrat and the newly liberated Negro offers an early and clear example of Tourgée's understanding—perhaps at times his misunderstanding—of post-bellum race relations" (35). Tourgée's concern with various "types" in the South—slave, slaveholder, and poor white—can be seen in A *Royal Gentleman.* But the parts set in the antebellum and war years suffer from the lack of direct observation which becomes the strength of Tourgée's Reconstruction novels. His lesser southern fictions include *John Eax and Mamelon; or, the South Without the Shadow* (New York: Fords, Howard, and Hulbert, 1882), and *Hot Plowshares* (New York: Fords, Howard, and Hulbert, 1883).

22. Gross, *Albion W. Tourgée,* 112.

23. In "The South as a Field for Fiction," *Forum,* VI (December, 1888), 404–13, Tourgée offered an explanation for why southern literature was currently dominating the literary market. He noted the intensity of the war experience for southern writers, the richness of settings, and character types like the Negro, the Confederate cavalier, and the poor white, as well as the romantic implications of the southern empire's downfall.

believes what they do not, and consequently undertakes what they never attempt. If he succeeds in his endeavor, the world stops laughing, and calls him a Genius: if he fails, it laughs the more, and derides his undertaking as A FOOL'S ERRAND."[24] Servosse Comfort, a thinly disguised Tourgée, is the fool of this novel. After serving in the Union army and fighting in the South, he moves his family to Warrington, a plantation in North Carolina. They are immediately enchanted with the beauty of the place, with "the balmy air, the unfamiliar land-scape, the strange sense of isolation which always marks the Southern plantation life" (FE, 38). Thus, from the opening of the novel the family's old home and the new land they have come to—the North and the South—are contrasted.

The northerners make their first "mistake" in their new home by inviting the Yankee schoolteachers from the "nigger" school to share Thanksgiving with them. Metta Servosse de-scribes the teachers as "cultivated, refined ladies of the best class of our Northern people, who have come here simply to do good" (FE, 42). In contrast, the local paper reports on the Thanksgiving dinner as follows: "The day itself is a relic of New-England Puritanical hypocrisy, and, we understand, was fitly observed at Warrington, where they ate and drank, and sung [sic] 'John Brown,' 'We're coming, Father Abraham,' and similar melodies. It is said that one of the 'N. T.'s.' [Nigger Teachers] became so full of the spirit of the occasion, that she kissed one of the colored boys who waited at the table. Colonel Servosse cannot expect his family to be recognized by respect-able people if he chooses such associates for them" (FE, 46).

Servosse further angers his white neighbors with his deci-sion to sell the land he does not need for his own living to

24. Albion W. Tourgée, *A Fool's Errand* (New York: Fords, Howard, and Hul-bert, 1879), [3]. Hereinafter, references to this work will be cited parenthetically in the text.

blacks who wish to become self-supporting farmers. As one native puts it, it seems that the Yankee colonel is determined to "put the niggers over the white folks" (*FE*, 47). When he is lured by his neighbors into making a speech at a political rally, Servosse advises them to abide by the outcome of the war. Addressing himself particularly to the questions of the war debt and Negro rights, he states, "There has been much discussion here today in regard to freedmen being allowed to testify in courts, the repudiation of the war-debt of these States, and one or two other kindred questions. Allow me to say that I think you are wasting your time in considering such matters. They are decided already" (*FE*, 55). Such statements arouse the wrath of his southern neighbors who feel they have suffered enough ill treatment from northerners. The speech provokes a physical attack and only the warning of a black friend enables Servosse to escape an ambush on his return home from the political meeting.

The numerous incidents of threats and violence throughout the novel illustrate the author's "look what is wrong here; see what needs to be done" theme. The most shocking is the cold-blooded murder of a union man, John Walters, for his political views. [25] Tourgée makes this figure heroic by suggest-

---

25. Tourgée incorporated three incidents reported in *Third Annual Message of W. W. Holden, Governor of North Carolina*, November, 1870, Doc. No. 1, Session 1870–71 (Raleigh: J. W. Holden, 1870), in *A Fool's Errand* and *Bricks Without Straw*. In *A Fool's Errand* the murder of John Walters and the hanging of Uncle Jerry are similar to the actual murder of Republican Senator John W. Stephens and the hanging of Negro Wyatt Outlaw. The burning of a Negro schoolhouse and church as reported in "Third Annual Message" is recounted in *Bricks Without Straw*. Tourgée uses the Stephens murder as source material, retaining such details as locale and method of murder, but he embellishes for dramatic effect. For example, Tourgée changes a report of bloodstains on the woodbox and walls of the room to a "single drop of blood" on the windowsill which gives Walters' followers a clue to the murder. He also appears to have added the scenes of Walters viewing his children playing on a nearby lawn. Although Tourgée drew on actual incidents, he used his creative powers as a writer to intensify his story.

ing that although he has worked hard for blacks, he is not concerned with personal power. Walters' decision to ignore the Ku Klux Klan warnings not to attend a political rally is fatal. His grisly murder is described by a black man who overheard one of the conspirators give an account of it:

Den dey turned him half over, all on us holdin' his arms an' legs, an' Jack Cannon stuck a knife inter his throat. He bled like a hog; but we caught de blood in a bucket, an' afterwards let it down out o' de winder in a bag to de fellers outside; so't der wa'n't a drop o' blood, nor any mark ub the squabble, in de room. We stowed him away in de wood-box, an', arter it comes on good an' dark, de boys are goin' to take him ober, an' stow him away under dat damned nigger schoolhouse o' his; an' den you see we'll claim de niggers done it, an' perhaps hev some on 'em up, an' try 'em for it! (FE, 198–99).

Tourgée drew this account from an actual murder of a state senator. The major elements of the incident are true, but the author added a few dramatic touches to make a compelling portrayal for his northern reading audience.

In the novel Tourgée repeatedly shows southerners as ignorant, hostile, backward, and provincial. But in doing so, to a degree at least, he explains their crimes. For, as he says several times, unlike their Northern white counterparts they do not really know better. Their thinking is bounded by more than a century of tradition and by the previously unchallenged assumptions that the black man is inferior and that the southern code has appropriately placed him in his servile, serflike role.

Thus, the novel's greatest villains are the northern politicians who after the brief period of Reconstruction turned their backs on blacks and, by not resisting, allowed the South to be "redeemed." There are no major characters who actively play this role, but by using such devices as letters and newspaper and journal articles Tourgée traces the change in thinking taking place after the conclusion of the war and points specifically to those politicians who are willing to accept short-term gains (such as southern support in elections) over the long-term goals for which the Civil War was fought. "We Republicans of the South will go down with the reconstruction movement," he predicts. "Some of us will make a good fight for the doomed craft; others will neither realize nor care for its danger: but on neither will justly rest the responsibility. That will rest now and for all time with the Republican party of the North,—a party the most cowardly, vacillating, and inconsistent in its management of these questions, that has ever been known in any government" (*FE*, 152). Tourgée's advocacy of northern support for reform in the South has been consistent throughout. But in the novel, much as in his own life, it becomes increasingly apparent that the North is not willing to continue the work it started. The author calls himself a fool because he continued with that work long after shrewder people, seeing it lacked profit, had desisted. *A Fool's Errand*, by casting real materials into an intense, fictionalized plot, shows what conditions were like in the South after the war and castigates a northern reading audience for neglecting the work still to be done there.[26]

This same theme, together with some concrete suggestions for reform, is present in *Bricks Without Straw* which appeared the following year. Turning from the semiautobiographical mode, Tourgée constructed in this novel a double plot: an

---

26. As has been noted by Gross and others, Tourgée's portrayal of the South is not always accurate. He emphasizes certain points (such as Klan activity) and ignores others. For example, he omits references to some Union League activities which were also illegal.

account of the fate of a black community attempting to assert its newly won rights of suffrage, education, and equal opportunity to pursue a livelihood, and a less convincing love story of former Confederate soldier and a Yankee schoolmarm.

Tracing the careers of two blacks, Nimbus Desmit and Eliab Hill, the author presents a combination of brawn and brains—Nimbus is rugged and an expert tobacco farmer; Eliab, a cripple, is instrumental in the growth of the free school for Negroes. The two, hoping by hard work and education to help uplift their fellow blacks, prosper as long as they have the protection of the law and recourse to the Freedman's Bureau for grievances. When the process of southern "redemption" begins, a band of Klansmen burn their church and savagely beat Eliab. Nimbus, after seeing that his friend is cared for, flees into the night, once again as poor as when he was a slave.

The love story is reminiscent of *Miss Ravenel's Conversion*, though in this case the girl is a Yankee and the man a southerner. Mollie Ainslie meets and falls in love with the Confederate Hesden Le Moyne, who fought in the southern army more from a sense of honor than to support the southern system. After returning from the war, Le Moyne lives with his mother and small son, keeping apart from political affairs. His encounter with Mollie, a Yankee schoolteacher at the Negro school, and Nimbus' plea that he care for Eliab Hill after a Klan attack on the black settlement, jolt him out of his isolation. When a neighbor, a Union man who has been whipped by Klansmen, asks for his help, Le Moyne is too honorable to refuse. He is at once ostracized by his neighbors and branded as a Radical. By the end of the novel Le Moyne's convictions are firm, and in a speech similar to Servosse's in *A Fool's Errand* he declares, "It is my sincere conviction that we ought to accept, in spirit as well as in form, the results of this struggle; not in part, but fully."[27]

Bricks Without Straw reinforces the thematic purposes of *A Fool's Errand*. The southern whites who cheat and plunder and coerce blacks into giving up the rights for which a long battle had been fought are wrong. Tourgée consistently pictures their false pride, intolerance, and brutality, making no attempt to excuse their actions. The Klan raid, for example, is presented in gory, vivid detail, enabling the reader to react fully to this crime.

But again the author emphasizes that there is a greater villain. If the South has acted odiously, it has acted in accordance with its traditions. If it has been barbaric, this barbarism has often been ingrained and unconscious. With the return of control to local governments the former rulers of the South saw an opportunity to regain power, and the North turned its back on those it should have protected. "The smouldering passion of the South had burst forth at last! For years—ever since the war—prejudice and passion, the sense of insult and oppression had been growing thicker and blacker all over the South. Thunders had rolled over the land. Lightnings had fringed its edges. The country had heard, but had not heeded. The nation had looked on with smiling face, and declared the sunshine undimmed" (*BWS*, 267–68). The North had held out a hope to the black man of freedom and equality; it had promised that its own democratic institutions would be available to the entire nation. But just when these changes were being implemented and men like Nimbus were, for the first

27. Tourgée, *Bricks Without Straw*, ed. Otto H. Olsen (Baton Rouge: Louisiana State University Press, 1969), 410. Hereinafter, references to this work will be cited parenthetically in the text.

time, developing into full-fledged men and citizens, the North withdrew its aid and turned away.

Hesden Le Moyne voices Tourgée's solution: "The *only* remedy, is to educate the people until they shall be wise enough to know what they ought to do, and brave enough and strong enough to do it" (*BWS*, 450). Significantly, Tourgée's spokesman is now a southerner. Probably the realization that northern policy would offer little support for racial equality in the South led him to hope that eventually the "better" class of southerners, represented here by Le Moyne, would take up the cause of freedom. Tourgée hoped that through universal education blacks would learn to control their future and that the southern whites would increasingly accept and respect them as fellow citizens. The title, *Bricks Without Straw*, suggests that freedom without education is a worthless commodity. Having witnessed the futility of the Negroes' attempts Tourgée wanted his fiction to encourage others to take note of their plight.

The themes of the novels of De Forest and Tourgée include a number of similarities. Through both explicit and implicit comparison, each portrayed northern democratic ideals as superior to those of the aristocratic, caste-ridden south. Both men indicated that southerners could learn much by modeling themselves after their northern neighbors. In these attitudes, the two writers reflect the dominant opinion of nonsoutherners immediately after the war. They viewed the Civil War as a holy war whose goals must be continued and strengthened.

De Forest's purpose ends at that point. Tourgée's longer experience in the South and his consequent observation of the two stages of postwar treatment gave him additional perspective. Like De Forest he viewed the South chiefly as a place that must be improved, literally "saved" through reform. But having witnessed the northern policy of "let them go their own way," he felt an added incentive to warn against what he considered a great northern mistake.

3.

The fiction of De Forest and Tourgée thus reflects northern attitudes toward the South immediately after the Civil War, mirroring the predominant opinion that the social and political system in the South was wrong and should be changed. But granted that these opinions were predominant in the North, if viewing the South as a prime target for reform were the only motivation for writers, certainly prose tracts outlining necessary changes would have been sufficiently instructive. The continued production and popularity of postwar fiction using southern themes point to more compelling appeals in the novels being written by such men as Tourgée and De Forest.

In *Cavalier and Yankee* William Taylor traces the search by American fiction writers for a national character. In the 1820s and 1830s they became concerned with creating a character that represented uniquely American values. Taylor traces the evolution of the transcendent Yankee character (as in Cooper's *The Spy*) into a legend positing a dual origin for the American national character—a combination of the cavalier and Yankee. As Americans became less content with what they viewed as the rather mundane characteristics of the present day democratic man—his avarice, his lack of gentility or cultivation—the concept of the southern gentleman became increasingly more appealing. Only a few characters such as a Washington were large enough to contain the best elements of both types, and hence the need for a legend, an ideal, continued to grow.[28] The South became the locus for this legen-

28. William R. Taylor, *Cavalier and Yankee: The Old South and American National Character* (New York: Harper and Row, 1961), 101, 250, 257.

dary fiction. It was in certain key ways different from the
North in its politics, social structure, and general lifestyle.

By the 1850s these ideas—the South as legend, as a place
where those ideals not realized in routine American life might
exist—were concrete images. Southern elements of chivalry,
noblesse oblige, and romance were appearing in a great deal of
mid-nineteenth-century American fiction. When De Forest
and Tourgée returned to the South after the war the need for
illusions of the ideal and the fantasy of a special place still
existed, accompanied by the desire to use the real elements
that would characterize local color fiction. Despite their conscious statements about inequities in the South, these writers
depicted the things that had been of interest to Americans
before the war and would become even more popular in the
eighties and nineties when attitudes toward the South became
less hostile and local color writers began to capitalize on the
region's uniqueness.

De Forest's essays in *A Union Officer in the Reconstruction*
illustrate this preoccupation, displaying the full range of
southern society from the ignorant black—"the man and
brother"—to the upper classes or "chivalrous Southrons." In
sketches and vignettes De Forest presents characters not much
different from stereotypes that had appeared in earlier fiction
dealing with the South. He concludes that "the Negroes
wasted much of their time in amusement. What with trapping
rabbits by day and treeing 'possums by night, dances which
lasted till morning, and prayer-meetings which were little better than frolics, they contrived to be happier than they had 'any
call to be,' considering their chances of starving to death."[29]

The poor white is exemplified by two women who seek aid
in the bureau major's office: "They were two tall, lank, un-

29. De Forest, *A Union Officer in the Reconstruction*, 99.

gainly women, one twenty-three, the other twenty-seven, dressed in dirty, grayish homespun, with tallow complexions, straight, light, dead hair, broad cheek bones, and singularly narrow foreheads. One of them was made a little more repulsive than the other by a deformed hand." These two repeat the question most often posed by women of this class: "'Anythin' for the lone wimmen?'"[30] In this scene De Forest illustrates the various evils—ignorance, sloth, backwardness—of the class he considered the lowest in the South's social structure. While furthering his thesis that the South would benefit from a conscious observation of northern society, the author in his use of dialect and portraiture anticipates the techniques of local color writing.

Despite the barriers thrown up to a Yankee Reconstruction officer, De Forest also managed to observe and write about the former ruling classes. These descriptions, too, contain both the legendary aspects of the earlier plantation novels and the nostalgia of local color writing. Of the "chivalrous Southrons" he says, "they are more simple than we, more provincial, more antique, more picturesque; they have fewer of the virtues of modern society, and more of the primitive, the natural virtues; they care less for wealth, art, learning, and the other delicacies of an urban civilization; they care more for individual character and reputation of honor."[31]

His sympathy for this class of people is apparent in the following passage which reveals, despite his opposition to slavery and injustice, a belief in the "might-have-been" aspect of the South:

I speak of the "chivalrous Southrons," the gentry, the educated, the socially influential, the class which before the war governed the

30. *Ibid.*, 49.
31. *Ibid.*, 173.

South, the class which may govern it again. Even if these people knew that they had been in the wrong they would still be apt to feel that their punishment exceeded their crime, because it was truly tremendous and reached many who could not be guilty. I remember a widowed grandmother of eighty and an orphan granddaughter of seven, from each of whom a large estate on the sea islands had passed beyond redemption, and who were in dire poverty. When the elder read aloud from a newspaper a description of some hundreds of acres which had been divided among Negroes, and said, "Chattie, this is your plantation," the child burst into tears. I believe that it is unnatural not to sympathize with this little plundered princess, weeping for her lost domains in fairyland.[32]

Although Tourgée, in his essay "The South as a Field for Fiction," also fastened upon the uniqueness of both the poor white and Negro as distinctly southern types, De Forest's preoccupation with the poor white seems greater, probably a result of his experiences in the Freedman's Bureau. In *Kate Beaumont* he relates the experiences of a young southern aristocrat, Randolph Armitage, at a lowdowners ball. Between leaving his plantation home and arriving at the cracker cabin Randolph's "manner and voice had become strangely degraded. . . . In place of his make-believe, yet gracious gentility and tenderness [toward his wife] there was a wild, reckless, animal-like excitement." The room is so crowded with this rough bunch that "even the wide-open doors and windows and chinks and the broad chimney could not carry off all the mephitic steam generated by this mob of unclean people." De Forest notes the uniqueness of the type: "To a New-Englander or a Pennsylvania Quaker fresh from the pacific, temperate, educated faces of his birth-land, it would not have seemed possible that these visages were American. The general caste of countenance was a lean and hardened wildness, like that of

32. *Ibid.*, 197.

Albanian mountaineers or Calabrian brigands. There were no stolid, square, bull-dog 'mugs'; everywhere you saw cleverness, or liveliness, or at least cunning; but it was the cleverness of a wolfish or foxy nature."[33] De Forest remarked once that he had never attended one of these cracker balls and in the scene described above he expresses a feeling of revulsion. Nevertheless, the reader is aware of the lure that drew Randolph Armitage to the spree and must wonder if De Forest was not somewhat intrigued himself.

Both writers treat the black man at length in their novels, and it is here that the "real" verges most quickly into the stereotype. More than De Forest, Tourgée attempted to create believable Negro characters. Unfortunately he was not able to sustain characterization, and his blacks are usually reduced to helpless creatures by the actions of the whites with whom they live. Tourgée's argument brought with it a paradox; he wished to show blacks as educable, but at the same time he felt it necessary to picture them as helpless in order to stress the urgent need for northern support. The old stereotypes fitted the latter portraiture, and many of his blacks resemble those of De Forest, who wasn't particularly interested in blacks, and those of later writers who chose to pursue the Negro stereotype for its quaintness.

De Forest in *Kate Beaumont* presents Cato, the faithful servant who is happy to polish his master's boots every morning and ration out his toddies. Major Scott is an emancipated black in *Miss Ravenel's Conversion*, but the author focuses on the humorous aspects of this preacher who has trouble limiting himself to one wife; it is clear that although Scott is a leader of his people, he is dependent upon the white protagonists Dr.

33. De Forest, *Kate Beaumont* (1872; State College, Pa.: Bald Eagle Press, 1963), 266.

Ravenel and Lt. Colburne. Neither of the black characters achieves the status of autonomous human being, and often such representations degenerate into the prewar concept of the black as a helpless, dependent child.

Taylor notes that most of the fiction written about the South before the war ignored those elements the South had in common with the North, since they didn't contribute to the legend. The same is true for the writings of De Forest and Tourgée. With the exception of the merchant-class characters, who are treated rather lightly in *Kate Beaumont,* De Forest spends little time writing about small-town life, which was similar to village life in the North. The small farmer and the independent unioner are given more space in Tourgée's works, as in the character of the unionist, John Walters, in *A Fool's Errand,* but this character takes second place to portrayals of poor whites and blacks and to that exotic species—the southern gentlemen and their ladies.

It is in their portrayal of this noble class that De Forest and Tourgée fully succumb to the tradition in fiction of the South as legend. This may be seen in *Kate Beaumont,* which has its setting in the prewar South and contains most of the elements of the old plantation novel—the stereotype darkies, the quaint crackers, and some of the finest adherents of the code duello to be portrayed in fiction. The rash young Tom Beaumont and the pensive Wallace McAlister epitomize the southern Hotspur and Hamlet. Much of the action revolves around questions of whether someone's honor has been sullied and, if so, who should challenge whom to a duel. In addition, the analogy of the love of a Beaumont girl and a McAlister youth to the Montague-Capulet feud suggests the author's concern with depicting nobility.

The main characters in this novel capture the dreamlike qualities of ideal southerners. Kate Beaumont is the representative southern belle—beautiful, obedient to the wishes of her father and brothers, and the object of many a young cavalier's attentions. Her grandfather Kershaw, who is said to share many of Kate's genteel qualities, combines the wisdom of old age with the charm of the southern gentleman. He is described as "one of those noble souls who look all their nobility. In youth he had been a very handsome man, and at eighty he was venerably beautiful. His massive aquiline face, strangely wrinkled into deep furrows which were almost folds, was a sublime composition of dignity, serenity, and benevolence." This countenance, says the author, "perfectly expressed his character. He was one of those simple, pure, honorable, sensible country gentlemen (of whom one meets more perhaps in our Southern States than in most other portions of this planet) who strike one as having a reserve of moral and intellectual power too great for their chances of action, and who lead one to trust that Washingtons will still be forthcoming when their country needs [them]." [34] Strengthening the fantasy element of this novel is the fact that finally the protagonist, Frank McAlister, abandons his notions of pursuing his profession of mineralogy in South Carolina and, after his marriage, is content to live as a planter, presumably happily ever after.

It seems clear that in De Forest's novel, *Miss Ravenel's Conversion from Secession to Loyalty,* the Yankee Colburne's capturing of the love of Lillie Ravenel parallels the capitulation of the South to the North. Although a number of the more admirable characters in the novel are northerners, the most interesting are southern. For example, the southerner Mrs. LaRue is evil, but also good-looking and charming; in contrast to her worldliness the simplicity of the heroine, Lillie

34. *Ibid.,* 139–40.

Ravenel, at times appears a trifle dull. Colonel Carter, the story's villain, is egotistical and a philanderer—but the reader, like Lillie, feels his personal magnetism. After all, like a true southern gentleman he can hold his liquor and command men. Although De Forest, in keeping with the moral of his story, was forced to make the southerner Carter lose out to the more temperate northern Colburne, he shows Carter to be gallant even in his ruin.[35] The colonel treats Lillie with unfailing courtesy, and he resorts to financial trickery only to provide his family with all the trappings of luxurious living. Certainly we cannot admire Carter, but in spite of ourselves we are charmed by him.

It has been noted earlier that in this novel De Forest used a southerner, Dr. Ravenel, to make the most telling pronouncements on southern vices. But despite his criticism of southern life, Dr. Ravenel himself embodies the best qualities of the southern ideal. He is in all ways a gentleman, truer even than Colonel Carter to all forms of courtesy toward women. He has cultivation, breeding, and a charm he employs successfully with his northern acquaintances. Readily entering the cliquish society of New Boston, he becomes a favorite at local gatherings: "The Doctor, travelled man of the world as he was, made no sort of difficulty in enjoying or seeming to enjoy these attentions. If he did not sincerely and heartily relish the New Bostonians, so different in flavor of manner and education from the society in which he had been educated, he at least made them one and all believe that they were luxuries to his palate. He became shortly the most popular man for a dinner party or an evening *conversazione* that was ever known

35. In *Fiction Fights the Civil War: An Unfinished Chapter in the Literary History of the American People* (Chapel Hill: University of North Carolina Press, 1957), Robert A. Lively notes that Colburne comes out second best. He wins a secondhand wife and his war has little romance about it.

in that city of geometry and puritanism" (MRC, 23). In Dr. Ravenel De Forest seems to present those genial qualities that might be lacking in a scholarly, frigid New Bostonian.

Although Tourgée makes fewer authorial comments concerning southern charm and gentility, those elements persistently intrude into his fiction, too. In *A Fool's Errand* it is likely that the hero Comfort Servosse's daughter will marry Melville Gurney, a reformed southern hothead who has the attributes of fine looks and good breeding. In the closing scenes of the novel, the death of the northern radical Servosse seems to be the author's fantasied version of his own death; it is fascinating that Servosse chooses to be surrounded by southern gentlemen who at last come together to wish him well, and he is even made to ask for their forgiveness and acceptance.

Bricks Without Straw is Tourgée's plea in fiction for education in the South. The ostensible heroes in this novel are the freedmen Nimbus Desmit and Eliab Hill and the northern-born schoolteacher, Mollie Ainslie. All three, however, are at one time or another dependent on the southern planter, Hesden Le Moyne, a character who is probably Tourgée's greatest contribution to the southern legend. Le Moyne, a romantic figure who has lost an arm in the war, lives in virtual seclusion with his mother and son. He has the proper aristocratic heritage, which is related by an acquaintance who speaks of Le Moyne's father: "He came from Virginia, and was akin to the Le Moynes of South Carolina, one of the best of those old French families that brag so much of their Huguenot blood. . . . They are a mighty elegant family; no doubt of that" (BWS, 50). Tourgée reserves for this southerner the honor of serving as a mouthpiece for his own educational philosophy. In much the same manner as De Forest in his treatment of Dr. Ravenel, Tourgée seems to feel that this ideal gentleman should be the spokesman for the thematic truths of his fiction—as if the magic of the legendary figure might lend strength to the author's purpose.

When Mollie Ainslie is forced to seek shelter from a storm at the Le Moyne plantation home, Mulberry Hill, Le Moyne's mother, Hester, asks Mollie to wear a splendid dress which she had worn as a young girl before the war. In a scene where the young schoolteacher and the two southerners sit together at dinner Tourgée evokes completely the aura of antebellum courtly life. They dine in a room where "the customary lamp had been banished, and colored wax-candles, brought from some forgotten receptacle, burned in the quaint old candelabra with which the mantels of the house had long been decorated" (BWS, 206). Thus, Mulberry Hill and its inhabitants retain, even if only as memories, the best elements culled from the plantation novels.

At the conclusion of *Bricks Without Straw* the heroine has been transformed from Mollie Ainslie, Yankee schoolmarm, to Mrs. Hesden Le Moyne, southern gentlewoman. She fears now that she may have misjudged the southern whites: "She began to feel as if she had done them wrong, and sought by every means in her power to identify herself with their pleasures and their interests." No longer mistress of the Negro school, she adapts the southern forms of charity in the best tradition of lady bountiful, and "rarely did a week pass that her carriage did not show itself in the little hamlet" on a visit to the school (BWS, 400). Both Hesden and Mollie have been transformed, and the result is that they come to possess the highest qualities of the southern aristocracy.

Each of the four novels discussed has stereotyped characters such as helpless or frolicking blacks; each portrays a dashing southern courtier who woos the hand of his lady. Both authors sing the praises of the southern gentleman and describe the elegant aspects of plantation life, made even more precious by the irreversible blow the war had dealt to this way of life. Thus, in plot, characterization, and theme Tourgée and De Forest acknowledge, even if unconsciously, the lure of the South both as real and ideal. In their evocation of the legendary aspects of the antebellum South and the nostalgia for a bygone era, these novels are a link between prewar southern novels and the local color and realistic writing that would appear in the eighties and nineties. Above all, these writers, though consciously speaking out against southern characteristics that had been praised before the war and would be admired again, were themselves continuing a tradition of evoking for a yearning reading public the legend of what "was *different* down there."

III

⟐

Constance Woolson and Southern Local Color

Unlike John W. De Forest and Albion Tourgée, who came to the South as agents of an occupying army and an outside government, Constance Fenimore Woolson's southern experience was voluntary and unconnected with politics. She came as a visitor and remained to form impressions she would turn into fiction. And she did not feel compelled either to be critical of southern life or to make suggestions for its reform.

Woolson was among a number of writers who, during the decades of the seventies and eighties, wrote what has been termed local color fiction, seeking to provide their reading audiences with pictures of a provincial life not yet deeply affected by the changes taking place in postwar America. Since the emphasis in this kind of fiction was primarily that of evoking the uniqueness of an unspoiled or out-of-the-way place, the setting received a greater amount of attention than did other elements. Characterization was used primarily for showing the quaintness of the inhabitants and tended to produce mere types. Adhering to the standards of genteel fiction favored by leading magazines such as *Atlantic*, *Harper's*, and the *Century*, most local color writing depended on a fairly conventional or romantic plot. Because characterization and plot were usually thin, it was difficult to sustain the texture or setting for great lengths and most local color writing thus took the form of short stories. Although some of these authors wrote novels, the plot deficiencies of the local color medium usually became apparent in the larger form.

Woolson's nomadic lifestyle prepared her well for local color writing. Although there have been conflicting accounts of the date of her birth, John Kern in his biography of Woolson convincingly defends the date as March 5, 1840.[1] She was born in Claremont, New Hampshire, the sixth daughter of Charles Jarvis Woolson and Hannah Cooper Pomeroy Woolson. Her father was descended from old New England families and her mother was a niece of Fenimore Cooper—a connection the author found helpful when beginning to publish her own works.

Soon after Woolson was born, three of her sisters died of scarlet fever, and to make a fresh start the family moved to Cleveland. Here Constance attended school and became familiar with the Ohio and Wisconsin region. In the summers the family vacationed at their cottage at Mackinac Island, which later became the setting for a number of her short stories. In 1858 she graduated from Madame Chegary's school in New York City and, journeying with her family, was presented in a number of fashionable resorts where she was reported to have been a great success. Upon the outbreak of the Civil War she worked for the Union cause and apparently had a brief romance with a Union officer who had been a childhood friend.[2]

---

1. John Dwight Kern, *Constance Fenimore Woolson: Literary Pioneer* (Philadelphia: University of Pennsylvania Press, 1934), 4. For additional biographical details see Clare Benedict (ed.), *Constance Fenimore Woolson* (London: Ellis, 1930), Vol. II of Clare Benedict (ed.), *Five Generations (1785–1923): Being Scattered Chapters from the History of the Cooper, Pomeroy, Woolson, and Benedict Families, with Extracts from the Letters and Journals, as well as Articles and Poems by Constance Fenimore Woolson* (3 vols.; London: Ellis, 1929–30). More recently, Rayburn S. Moore has published a biography entitled *Constance F. Woolson* (New Haven: College and University Press, 1963).

2. Kern, *Woolson*, 5, 6. See also Moore, *Constance F. Woolson*, 23, 24.

Already she knew the Great Lake country and New York. After her father's death in 1869 she became her mother's constant companion and began the nomadic existence that for the remainder of her life would take her to various parts of the South and Europe where she observed and wrote about what she saw. By 1870 when regional literature was becoming extremely popular and Bret Harte's *Luck of Roaring Camp and other Stories* was in vogue, Woolson was already well prepared to satisfy the demand for regional stories. [3]

Woolson and her mother traveled extensively in the eastern part of the United States between New York and St. Augustine, often accompanied, after her husband's death, by Clare Benedict, Woolson's sister. Enroute to St. Augustine the three women visited New York, Philadelphia, Washington, Richmond, Charleston, and Jacksonville, the sisters arming themselves with guidebooks to gain more information about the southern cities they visited. Between 1873 and 1879, however, Woolson and her mother spent most of their time in the Carolinas and Florida, and the author thus gained her knowledge of the South through more than brief visits.

After the death of their mother in 1879, Woolson and Benedict sailed for Europe, landing in Liverpool and from London going to France. By 1880 they were in Florence. The remainder of Constance Woolson's life would be spent abroad where she visited most of the capitals, became a friend of Henry James, and continued her writing of short stories based largely on her Italian experience. [4] From 1890 to 1893 she

3. Kern, *Woolson*, 9.
4. For a discussion of the relationship between Woolson and Henry James see Leon Edel, *Henry James: The Middle Years, 1882–1895* (Philadelphia: J. B. Lippincott, 1962). Edel supplies evidence to indicate that, on Woolson's part at least, the relationship between the two might have been more than just friendship and notes that James apparently felt that in failing to recognize or respond to Woolson's feel-

lived in England, leaving Oxford in the spring of 1893 for Italy. On January 24, 1894, she died in Venice, having either fallen or leapt from her bedroom window and never regaining consciousness. Accounts of her death vary; some attribute it to delirium resulting from influenza, others to the culmination of a continuing depression.[5] At the time of her death she had achieved a moderate degree of recognition as a writer; today her works are virtually unknown.

The traveling Constance Fenimore Woolson did in America, visiting the Great Lakes, the Deep South, and Florida, gave her ample opportunity to observe parts of the country that were unlike the urban Northeast and were ideal subjects for local color. Her accounts of these places appeared as short stories published in magazines, and her fiction gained a large reading audience. Most of her best writing appears in such short stories as those collected in *Rodman the Keeper: Southern Sketches.* Her novels often fail to sustain three-dimensional characterization, and plots which might be credible in shorter form appear overly contrived or even ludicrous when drawn out for several hundred pages.

Like other writers of local color fiction, Woolson attempted to capture in her work the uniqueness of the places about which she wrote—to value their differences rather than to urge their conformity with the rest of the nation. This approach reflected a general attitude in an American society whose zeal for reform had diminished since the years immediately after the war. Northerners were beginning to realize the expediency of being less harsh with southerners and were increasingly disenchanted with Reconstruction politics.

---

ings, he was responsible in part for her death. In his preface to *Constance F. Woolson* Rayburn Moore states his reservations about Edel's conclusions.

5. Kern, *Woolson,* 161.

Where Tourgée and De Forest saw prejudice and inequal-
ities, Woolson singled out unique customs and traditions.
And though their fiction focuses on a number of the same
elements, their differing attitudes were not just personal
but seemed to reflect a changing climate of opinion in the
nation.

The stories published between 1875 and 1880—for the
most part written while Woolson was in the South—draw
entirely on southern settings and themes. Her novels, which
were written later, also treat southern elements. All in all she
wrote some fifteen short stories based on various parts of the
South, as well as a number of travel sketches, one novelette,
and three novels set either entirely or largely in the South.

Most of the short stories involve an assortment of characters, northern and southern, placed in intricately constructed,
contrived plots. Although she often protested that she was
writing realistically—and her readers frequently criticized the
stories for lacking happy endings—most of them are typical of
the genteel fiction of the eighties in their inclusion of authorial comments on propriety and in the preponderance of characters who seem isolated from the baser things of life. The
realism in her stories, as with other writers of the local color
school, derives largely from her careful descriptions of place
which create the impression that the author has superimposed
the tale upon a very realistic setting.

This delicate etching of details makes her settings much
easier to visualize than those of De Forest and Tourgée. Un-
concerned with persuading her audience to reform, Woolson
concentrated on picturing the South about which she was
writing. In contrast to De Forest, who used setting chiefly as a
backdrop for his stories and sketches, and Tourgée, in whose
works the setting is often sketchy and sometimes conspicu-
ously absent, Woolson painstakingly evokes the uniqueness of

each of her locales. The result is a pervasively thorough description of Florida, the Carolina mountains, and the lowlands, as in the short story "In the Cotton Country" where the description of the land is subtly linked with her admiration for the spirit of the people: "Accustomed to the trim, soldierly ranks of the Western corn-fields, or the billowy grace of the wheat, I could think of nothing save a parade of sturdy beggarmen unwillingly drawn up in line, when I gazed upon the stubborn, uneven branches and generally lop-sided appearance of these [cotton] plants. . . . But after a while I grew accustomed to their contrary ways, and I even began to like their defiant wildness." [6] For Woolson, as for other local color writers, the description of place was often an end in itself.

In contrast to her treatment of setting, the development of characterization in Woolson's stories and novels is often superficial and stereotyped. For example, none of her black characters rises above a conventional portrait. The faithful black slave who serves his Confederate soldier master in Woolson's "Rodman the Keeper" retains the devotion exhibited by Peyton Beaumont's valet in De Forest's *Kate Beaumont*. De Forest's novel, however, is set in pre-Civil War times, making the portrait of a servile, docile slave at least palatable to his audience. Woolson presents the very same kind of childlike lackey stereotype in a postwar setting. In "Old Gardiston" an old Negro couple remain with their former owners, showing no desire to embark upon a new life. The author even suggests that the blacks' attempts to earn money in order to ward off starvation for the white family is a form of heroism. But here, as in her other stories, the characters are never individualized; they remain merely a charming part of the setting.

6. Constance Fenimore Woolson, "In the Cotton Country," *Appleton's Journal,* XV (April 29, 1876), 547.

Woolson's treatment of blacks in "King David," the story of a young New Englander who fails in his venture to establish a freedom school, reflects an attitude very unlike Tourgée's concerning education of the newly liberated slaves. She rejects the idea of salvation by means of the schoolhouse. The blacks in this story fall into two classes: those who are too dull to learn, and those who have intelligence but use it to seek more immediate gratification such as getting drunk and terrorizing whites. It is a pessimistic story and a convincing argument in support of the growing national sentiment that it was time to let the South again take up the management of its own affairs.

The contrast in this story between David's restless students and the old servant of the southern planter Mars Ammerton makes clear the distance between Woolson's position and that presented by Tourgée in his hopeful portrayals of eager black students. Woolson's blacks could never be educated into equality with whites; and the author implies that for blacks the role of servant is more appropriate than that of student. Even David is forced to acknowledge the contrast between the servant and his master: "There sat the planter, his head crowned with silver hair, his finely chiseled face glowing with the warmth of his indignant words; and there passed the old slave, bent and black, his low forehead and broad animal features seeming to typify scarcely more intelligence than that of the dog that followed him." [7] By the time Woolson came to the South, the northern ardor for black education had been dampened, and, not concerned with provoking social reform, she capitalized on a portrayal of blacks that, perhaps unintentionally, helped to salve the conscience of the nation. In two

---

7. Constance Fenimore Woolson, "King David," *Scribner's*, XV (April, 1878), reprinted in *For the Major and Selected Short Stories*, ed. Rayburn S. Moore (New Haven: College and University Press, 1967), 112.

separate, extended analogies in which blacks are compared with dogs, she implies that letting southerners take control of their government would, in a sense, merely be restoring ever-faithful Old Dog Tray to his much-needed master.

In Woolson's works the treatment of the poor white is also slight, since for her this class was simply not good romantic material.[8] In her few accounts of poor whites she maintains a feeling of great distance between the narrator and these characters, suggesting that she had little opportunity to come in contact with and observe them. When they do appear it is usually as a specialized type of a colorful or exotic nature—the mountain moonshiners or the Minorcans of Florida.

In her writings about Florida, especially in "Felipa,"[9] the story of a young Minorcan girl who worships the wealthy northerners vacationing at her beach, and *East Angels,* in which Minorcans are presented as servants and villagers, Woolson incorporates the poor whites as local color elements. These people are interesting for their unusual dialect (a mixture of Spanish, English, and other tongues), their ties to the sea where they make their living as fishermen, and their simple, almost idyllic life. None of Woolson's upper-class characters (around whom most of her plots are centered) ever becomes very involved with the Minorcans; instead, their value is in adding variety to the stories and providing a contrast to the complex northern society the author juxtaposes with the slower-paced South. There is little criticism in the portrai-

8. *Ibid.* Woolson was obviously repelled by the poor whites of the Piedmont and coastal areas of the Carolinas and Georgia. She refers to David King as being "spared the sight of their long, clay-colored faces, lank yellow hair, and half-open mouths; he was not brought into contact with the ignorance and dense self-conceit of this singular class" (110).

9. Constance Fenimore Woolson, "Felipa," *Lippincott's Magazine,* XVII (June, 1876), 702–13.

tures. Woolson includes them occasionally because, like the palm trees, sandy beaches, and flamingoes, they are interesting.

More than anything else these writers who came to the South were intrigued by the very different way of life epitomized by upper-class southerners. And Woolson, unlike the earlier "reform" writers, was free to extol every southern virtue available and to capitalize on each unique aspect of a passing way of life; this was, indeed, what her audience expected. In two of her most popular stories, "Old Gardiston" and "Rodman the Keeper," Woolson fulfilled the expectations of her readers by presenting compelling accounts of the passing of a finer way of life. Both stories take place immediately after the Civil War, before the restoration of southern control. In "Rodman the Keeper" the author contrasts a young Union veteran and his Yankee ways with remnants of the old order. Unlike the optimism of Tourgée's fiction, there is in the story little hope of a better future for southerners. Hoping to restore his shattered health, John Rodman returns to the South after the war as keeper of a federal cemetery and encounters a wounded Confederate soldier, tended only by a faithful servant, who has returned home to die in his ancestral mansion. The story is presented from Rodman's point of view and the reader's sympathy is directed toward Rodman's generosity to his former enemies as he takes over the care of the wounded soldier. But the author's greatest preoccupation is with creating a vivid picture of the desolation of a once noble land, and she achieves this effect in an account of the soldier's funeral: "They carried him home to the old house, and from there the funeral started, a few family carriages, dingy and battered, following the hearse, for death revived the neighborhood feeling; that honor at least they could pay—the sonless mothers and the widows who lived shut up in the old

houses with everything falling into ruin around them, brood-
ing over the past."[10] At the conclusion of the story Rodman
observes a fellow Yankee engaged in tearing down the old
mansion. Woolson's point, made clear by showing it through
the realization of another Yankee, is that what is going on
here is regrettable, and she reiterates this belief in other
stories.

In "Old Gardiston" Woolson continues her idealization of
the eclipsed order by presenting the plight of an old family
immersed in the deepest reaches of poverty and literally sub-
sisting on pride—in its past, and in the few shabby possessions
still retained that hearken back to a brighter era. The point of
view in the story is that of Gardis Duke, a young girl who lives
with her ancient Cousin Copeland in the old Gardiston mansion with only two loyal servants to help her manage the
estate. When soldiers from a Union regiment encamped on
their property protect them from an uprising of blacks, Gardis
is faced with the problems of repaying them in the face of two
obstacles—her well-developed hatred of Yankees and poverty
so obvious that it will require all her ingenuity to provide a
decent dinner for the two commanding officers of the regiment.

Gardis wishes to emulate her late aunt, who in the midst of
ruin had valiantly invited two other "ancient dames" to make
a visit of several days according to the old ways. She had
admired "the state the three kept together in the old drawing
room under the family portraits, the sweep of their narrow-
skirted, old-fashioned silk gowns on the inlaid staircase when
they went down to dinner, the supreme unconsciousness of
the breakneck condition of the marble flooring and the mold-

10. Constance Fenimore Woolson, *Rodman the Keeper: Southern Sketches* (New
York: D. Appleton, 1880), reprinted in *For the Major*, ed. Moore, 101.

streaked walls, the airy way in which they drank their tea out of the crocodile cups, and told little stories of fifty years before." [11]

She gathers together all her forces for the dinner she feels compelled to give the officers out of a sense of "noblesse oblige," and it is a success in spite of the fact that the only dinner dress she has to wear is one that belonged to her great-grandmother and that there are not enough silver forks and spoons left to be used in company. She is able to present at least a semblance of the old order. Dinner is served in the lofty dining room, and the guests take coffee from the crocodile cups in the drawing room while Gardis sings for them. Having fulfilled her obligation according to southern customs, Gardis burns the dress she has worn to entertain Yankees.

As in "Rodman the Keeper" Woolson suggests that the old order is indeed passing, and, more importantly, that it can never really be possessed by the Yankees who speculate in purchases in the South. For when Gardis realizes that there is no longer enough money on which to live, she sells the house to a northern contractor's wife. Before the woman can take possession, however, it burns, "as though it knew a contractor's wife was waiting for it. 'I see our Gardis is provided for,' said the old house. 'She never was a real Gardiston—only a Duke; so it is just as well. As for that contractor's wife, she shall have nothing; not a Chinese image, not a spindle-legged chair, not one crocodile cup—no, not even one stone upon another." [12] Woolson's work projects a terrible sense of loss; the destruction of the past is regrettable, she implies, especially because no one can ever have it again. Southerners here are not

11. Constance Fenimore Woolson, "Old Gardiston," *Harper's*, LII (April, 1876), reprinted in *For the Major*, ed. Moore, 50.
12. *Ibid.*, 75–76.

getting their just deserts, as is sometimes implied by De Forest and Tourgée; their losses, in Woolson's picture, are tragic.

Because Woolson's treatment of the South has a broader base than that of Tourgée or De Forest—she was equally well versed in the ways of the southern lowland the two men treated and in the life of the mountains and Florida—her presentation of the lives of the natives is much more varied. Not satisfied with portraying the "might-have-been" aspect of a war-torn South, she went beyond De Forest and Tourgée to project this idealized life of the nobility, in a somewhat altered form, in the mountains of Carolina. Her novelette, *For the Major*, transposes the standard of noblesse oblige and gentility in the face of poverty into a setting where it might presumably continue to flourish. It is as if Woolson, having whetted the appetite of her readers by her sympathetic accounts of the Old South, hoped to persuade them through the Carroll family that such a life might still exist, although, of course, far from the crowded, industrial North. *For the Major* recounts the efforts of Madame Carroll, aided by her stepdaughter, Sara, to shield Major Carroll from the knowledge that he is growing old and infirm. This situation may be seen as a metaphor for all of Far Edgerly; the inhabitants of this town high in the mountains are also shielded from the encroaching world outside. The villagers, in fact, are proud of their isolation, although "there would seem to have been little in these lacks upon which to found a pride, if the matter had been viewed with the eyes of that spirit of progress which generally takes charge of American towns; but, so far at least, the Spirit of Progress had not climbed Chillawassee Mountain, and thus Far Edgerly was left to its prejudiced creed."[13] What a con-

13. Woolson, "For the Major," in *For the Major*, ed. Moore, 259.

trast to Comfort Servosse's comments in *A Fool's Errand,* as he anxiously awaits a flood of industrial immigration for the purpose of building a New South!

The Carrolls, as the aristocrats of the village, are the embodiment of the proud spirit which disdains the material progress already touching the neighboring village. Their weekly Sundays at home, their refined habits, their lineage, traced to a prosperous antebellum family from the sea islands, serve as a model to the entire village. Even its most respected institution, the church, cannot begin its weekly service until the Carrolls arrive, heralded by the clanking of the steps that are lowered from their ancient carriage: "The steps came down with a long clatter. . . . But no one in Far Edgerly would have sacrificed them for such trifles as these; they were considered to impart an especial dignity to 'the equipage' (which was, indeed, rather high-hung). No other carriage west of the capital had steps of this kind. It might have been added that no other carriage east of it had them either. But Chillawassee did not know this, and went on contentedly admiring." [14]

At the conclusion of the story Major Carroll does become senile, and Madame Carroll, who for years has been pretending to be what she is not (young, when she is old), strips away her paints, her blonde curls, and her white, girlish frock. This, however, is ironic, for Madame Carroll's actions have no thematic parallel in the story. Having wholeheartedly caught up the idealized presentation of a finer life—something at which De Forest and Tourgée had only hinted—Woolson sustains this illusion throughout her remaining work.

A corollary for the idealization of life in the South is, of course, the admiration for the so-called southern aristocrats who led such lives. If De Forest and Tourgée were unaware of

14. *Ibid.,* 261.

how much they praised southerners in their fiction, often as if between the lines, Woolson, in contrast, made few overt criticisms of her southerners. If she had misgivings, they were never voiced as explicitly as were those of De Forest and Tourgée. For she could not say enough about the fineness of these noble people to whom the war had dealt an unjust blow. Henry James remarked upon the "voicelessness" of the conquered South after the war; Woolson took up the voice of protest for the defeated.[15] In her portrayal of the planter Ammerton in "King David," for example, she sympathizes with a man of intelligence and breeding who is forced to submit to the political rule of ignorant, unruly blacks. His statement to the Yankee schoolmaster, David King, that he and other planters will band together to protect their interests, in such a context seems entirely justified.

Other such characters from Woolson's stories come swiftly to mind. Cousin Copeland in "Old Gardiston," who has spent his life in quiet pursuit of antiquarian study and is now thrust by forces over which he has no control into seeking employment as a clerk, becomes an object of our sympathy. When he is told, "We don't care for that kind of writing; it is old fashioned," we and the narrator mourn the fact that in the Reconstruction South the old ways are shunted aside and replaced by commercial values. Similarly, when Ward De Rossett of "Rodman the Keeper" dies and his young cousin Bettina Ward must seek her own living as a schoolteacher, possessing only "her poor armor of pride," we somehow agree with the author that these people who led fine lives should not be reduced to such circumstances. Woolson was protesting strongly to a now-sympathetic audience. For many in the

15. Henry James, "Miss Woolson," in *Partial Portraits* (London: Macmillan, 1888), 180.

North had come to agree with her: "What with the graves down in the South, and the taxes up in the North, they [northerners] were not prepared to hear any talk about beginning. Beginning, indeed! They called it ending. The slaves were freed, and it was right they should be freed; but Ethan and Abner were gone, and their households were left unto them desolate." [16] Let the South now take care of itself; and further, wasn't it now time to listen to the conscience of the nation, to question whether all the right lay only with one side?

This is not to say that Woolson was a political writer. Her concern was with fiction, with describing the land as she saw it, translated into the form of stories that would hold her readers' interest. But her descriptions, presented so vividly, were every bit as effective politically as had been Tourgée's impassioned plea just a few years earlier for those reforms Woolson was now deploring. The term "local color writer" has come to mean one who describes and appreciates the peculiar aspects of a particular area; functioning in this role, Woolson was writing at the ideal time to help capture for the South the sympathy of the nation.

One of the most dramatic examples of the attitudes reflected in Woolson's work may be seen in her use of the North-South romance. Because she began writing about the South when the necessity to be critical and to urge reforms no longer existed, it is understandable that her handling of this motif would be unlike that of the reform writers whose southern characters capitulated to northern lovers. Coming as she did to describe and praise, not to convert, there was no need for Woolson's southerners to capitulate to northern lovers. A romantic theme typical of her short stories and novels shows

16. Woolson, "King David," reprinted in *For the Major,* ed. Moore, 106.

the southerner as a beautiful young girl, very similar to De Forest's Lillie Ravenel, although perhaps more indolent. The northerner is usually a wealthy man, always older, often self-made, who is fascinated by the girl's charm and languor. In many cases an older northern woman lends a triangle aspect to the story. This triangle also appears in *Miss Ravenel's Conversion,* but Woolson avoids De Forest's expedient of killing off the third party. In a few stories, such as "Black Point" where the story is presented from the northern woman's point of view, the northerner wins her man after he ends a brief flirtation with the southern girl. This, however, is the exception in Woolson's work.

Horace Chase (1894) depicts a North-South romance of sorts. Ruth Franklin, an indolent, self-centered, and beautiful young girl, is wooed by the self-made northern millionaire Horace Chase. Although Chase is extremely generous to the impoverished Franklin family, Woolson never lets us forget that in spite of his kindnesses he is common. One of his first acts of courtship is to send flowers to L'Hommedieu, Ruth's home in Asheville. When Ruth's family breaks out in peals of laughter at the card, addressed "Lommy Dew," Chase explains, "I don't speak French myself. I thought perhaps it had something to do with dew." [17]

The marriage takes place, but Ruth soon falls in love with Walter Willoughby, a more refined young northerner who is ambitious but takes pride in the fact that he is not, like Chase, a drudging money-maker. When Ruth, realizing that Walter has no serious intentions about her and is, in fact, engaged to someone else, confesses to Horace, he does not presume to judge her—"Have I been so faultless myself that I have any

17. Constance Fenimore Woolson, *Horace Chase* (New York: Harper and Brothers, 1894), 32.

right to judge *you?*" [18] Although a reconciliation of sorts is achieved between husband and wife, it can hardly be called a capitulation of southerner to northerner.

We must also consider that Ruth's family is southern only by kinship to Mrs. Franklin's mother, a North Carolinian to whose home the Franklin family had moved some five years before the opening of the story. In the sense, then, that Ruth simply lives in the South and is not a native of it, *Horace Chase* is not the best example of Woolson's use of the North-South romance motif. For that we must turn to her best-known novel, *East Angels*, which illustrates her most extensive exploration into the relationship between North and South.

East Angels was written in 1884 and set in the St. Augustine area that Woolson loved, she said, better than any other place in America. To bring northerners and southerners into juxtaposition in the novel she employed the conventional plot technique of having a group of wealthy northerners, tired of the usual watering places, come to the little village of Gracias-á-Dios (St. Augustine) near the St. Johns River. Here Evert Winthrop, a native of New York and a self-made millionaire, meets and falls in love with Garda Thorne, young, poor, and as indolent as her tropical surroundings. Garda and her widowed mother live in the ancestral home of her father's family, a beautiful if crumbling villa set in the middle of an orange grove.

Garda, it becomes clear, is in need of a husband who can give her the advantages her mother cannot afford. Evert Winthrop is in a position to have almost any woman he might choose. Since the author had no moral comment to make, and no concessions were necessary on the part of her northern

18. *Ibid.*, 419.

and southern characters, it seems that she might have chosen to bring these proper beginnings of a love story to the logical conclusion of marriage. The story, however, doesn't work out in this manner. One immediate explanation is that without any complication to impede the romance Woolson may not have had enough material for a full-length novel, though complications could have been introduced and then resolved. Instead, the conclusion of the story is sad; Garda is dismissed as a woman who will undoubtedly have several husbands, and Evert Winthrop will live out his life unfulfilled by love. These results pivot around the introduction of the character, Margaret Harold, Evert's cousin by marriage, who is an example of Woolson's ideal northern woman.

Margaret has come to Gracias-á-Dios as the companion of her husband's aunt and, in contrast to Garda, is pursuing a life of self-sacrifice and denial. Deserted by her husband, she nevertheless assumes the blame for the failure of her marriage. As the story progresses we learn that she loves Evert Winthrop, but she rejects the possibility of divorce from her husband and, in Henry James's words, becomes a perfect example of self-immolation.[19] Conceding that it is necessary to give Margaret an opportunity to reject her one chance for happiness—a proposal by Evert—in order to present her as an ideal type who is strong enough to sacrifice all for honor's sake, the question of the abortive love affair between Garda Thorne and Evert Winthrop remains to be solved.

Woolson could have written a well-constructed story in which Evert, after finding Margaret unobtainable, continued pursuing his love for Garda, which is never convincingly extinguished in the novel. Margaret would still have her sacrifice intact, and there could have been a happy ending, as in the

19. James, "Miss Woolson," 189.

novels discussed earlier. But since Woolson was not overtly making criticisms of southern ways, it would not have been logical to reform Garda into a more appropriately serious woman such as Margaret. Even more importantly, the characterization of Garda Thorne embodies some of the very qualities local color writers were describing to evoke nostalgia in their urban reading audiences—things Woolson has shown as being virtually unobtainable. For example, Garda is of noble blood, and even though poor (like all the South), she is living in an idyllic manner unique to her section of the country. She becomes then, in the novel, an ideal; had she married Evert, the ideal would have been besmirched by reality—for there is no doubt that with his millions, Evert represents the wealthy industrial North. The idealization of nobility seen earlier in such stories as "Old Gardiston," with the repeated suggestions that this nobility is inaccessible to northerners who attempt to possess it but end by only mutilating or destroying it, is reinforced here by the fact that Evert cannot win Garda.

Garda lives in a part of paradise: "Gracias-á-Dios is very far from New Bristol. . . . It's all the difference between a real place and an ideal one." Garda, then, represents not only the beauty and elusiveness that is the South; she also becomes a symbol of an idealized existence, of an escape from reality. And Evert Winthrop, representative of that reality in which Woolson's readers lived, could be lured by this escape but could never possess it. If we see Garda as a symbol of "what might have been" and Evert as "reality," then Margaret Harold comes to symbolize the sort of rejection we all must make of an escapism we may dream of but can never achieve.

Other aspects of Garda's character support these conclusions—her light-heartedness, her very apparent sexuality which reflects the sensuality of a balmy, tropical land, her self-centeredness and rejection of all practical concerns (in contrast to the pragmatism of De Forest and Tourgée)—all these culminate to make her Woolson's single, strongest symbol of the idealized, escapist lure of the South. Under these circumstances there can be no reconciliation between northerner and southerner; one cannot possess or reform an ideal.

Although it has been suggested that De Forest and Tourgée were attracted to this idealized, escapist, "might-have-been" aspect of the South, De Forest's confidence in the superiority of the North and Tourgée's single-minded espousal of practical reforms kept them from being side-tracked into an evocation of the South as paradise. Woolson, not hampered by such reins, plunged ahead into a portrayal of the South as a might-be land, perhaps eluding possession but always remaining as a possibility. She represents a second step in the postwar treatment of the region by northerners, for in her work the South moves closer to becoming what was fleetingly suggested by De Forest and Tourgée, the mythical place needed by all men as a counterpoint to reality.

The South, which had been depicted in abolitionist literature as a charnel house of savagery and sensuality, and in the work of postwar northerners such as De Forest and Tourgée as a region characterized by questionable morality, rashness, and self-indulgence, becomes in the writing of Constance Woolson the land of milk and honey, the unspoiled Eden of a preindustrial world, a place that northerners cursed with the work ethic and the puritan scruple might dream about and view from afar, but never enter. No more do warnings abound that the South is in dire need of an immediate political and social—even moral—overhaul. Rather, the indolence, the sensuousness of a more relaxed life, the very unprogressiveness, become for the urbanizing, industrializing, materialistic Yankee a veritable rebuke.

IV

Lafcadio Hearn's Southern Paradise

In 1877 a Cincinnati, Ohio, newspaperman, nearly blind in one eye and facing difficulties at home, visited New Orleans and was enthralled. "I cannot say how fair and rich and beautiful this dead South is," he wrote to a friend back home. "It has fascinated me. I have resolved to live in it; I could not leave it for that chill and damp Northern life again." To a far greater extent than Constance Woolson or the other writers discussed earlier, Lafcadio Hearn's interest in the South was based frankly on its exoticism. Hearn was no moralist; as a writer social problems interested him little if at all; he sought atmosphere, climate, mood, attempting to find in art the order and meaning that eluded him in real life.

In large part, Hearn's ability to view the South as he did was the result of his far more varied background. He was not, to begin with, a native American at all. Born on the Isle of Santa Maura (Leucadia) off the west coast of Greece, the second son of Charles Hearn, a British army physician, and Rose Cassimati, a native Ionian, Hearn was educated in Ireland, England, and France. The financial ruin of his father's family ended his prospects among them, and in 1869 he went to America.[1]

1. For an introduction to Hearn's life see Elizabeth Stevenson's *Lafcadio Hearn* (New York: Macmillan, 1961). This is one of the more recent and most sympathetic biographical accounts of Hearn. There are numerous others, including Elizabeth

74

Hearn lived in Cincinnati from 1869 to 1877 and these were formative years for him. Here he made friends such as Henry Watkin, a printer who would remain important in his life, first for helping him secure a job and later as a sympathizer for his projects. Hearn entered into bustling, postwar American life and as a reporter for the *Enquirer* and *Commercial* began to develop a writing style that even much later retained traces of journalism. His innate curiosity, as well as a familiarity with street life, made him a natural for the sensational reporting of the day. Perhaps the most spectacular example of this is Hearn's November 9, 1874, account in the Cincinnati *Enquirer* of the infamous Tanyard murder. Hearn reconstructs the murder of Hermann Schilling, a night watchman burned alive in a furnace: "Fancy the shrieks for mercy, the mad expostulation, the frightful fight for life, the superhuman struggles for existence—a century of agony crowded into a moment—the shrieks growing feebler—the desperate struggles dying into feeble writhings. And through all the grim murderers, demoniacally pitiless. . . . Peering into the furnace until the skull exploded and the steaming body burst, and the fiery flue hissed like a hundred snakes!"[2]

In Cincinnati, the camaraderie of the group of reporters supplied a fellowship he had long missed and served as a consolation to the frustration of doing what must have seemed to him hackwork. In addition, the liberty he was given in adding authorial touches to his reports of the seamy side of the city allowed him to experiment with various forms of writing. At

---

Bisland's, *The Life and Letters of Lafcadio Hearn* (2 vols.; Boston: Houghton Mifflin, 1906). See also Edward Larocque Tinker, *Lafcadio Hearn's American Days* (New York: Dodd, Mead, 1924), and Beongcheon Yu, *An Ape of Gods: The Art and Thought of Lafcadio Hearn* (Detroit: Wayne State University Press, 1964).

2. Lafcadio Hearn, "Violent Cremation," in *An American Miscellany: Articles and Stories Now First Collected*, ed. Albert Mordell (2 vols.; New York: Dodd, Mead, 1924), I, 36–37.

this time he also had a fling at editing a short-lived weekly newspaper, *Ye Giglampz*, with H. F. Farny, and he began translations of such writers as Gautier and Flaubert.[3]

But by 1877 Hearn was tired of his life in Ohio. Increasing frustration with the rigors of reporting as well as his sensitivity to the disapproval he met from a liaison with a mulatto woman, led him to follow his dream of going South. His first impressions of New Orleans where he arrived after a short stay in Memphis fulfilled his expectations. In a letter to Henry Watkin he wrote: "The wealth of a world is here—unworked gold in the ore, one might say; the paradise of the South is here, deserted and half in ruins."[4] Later, in the opening paragraph of an article published in *Century Magazine* for November, 1883, Hearn looked back on his first view of New Orleans and made even more explicit both the contrast it offered to the North and the nature of its peculiar charms:

When I first viewed New Orleans from the deck of the great steamboat that had carried me from gray northwestern mists into the tepid and orange-scented air of the South, my impressions of the city, drowsing under the violet and gold of a November morning, were oddly connected with memories of *Jean-ah Poquelin*. That strange little tale and its exotic picturesqueness had considerably influenced my anticipations of the Southern metropolis, and prepared me to idealize everything peculiar and semitropical that I might see. Even before I had left the steamboat my imagination had already flown beyond the wilderness of cottonbales, the sierra-shaped roofs of the sugar-sheds, the massive fronts of refineries and storehouses, to wander in search of the old slave-trader's mansion, or at least of something resembling it.[5]

3. Théophile Gautier, *One of Cleopatra's Nights and Other Fantastic Romances,* trans. Lafcadio Hearn (New York: R. Worthington, 1882).

4. Lafcadio Hearn, *Letters from the Raven: Being the Correspondence of Lafcadio Hearn with Henry Watkin,* ed. Milton Bronner (New York: Albert and Charles Boni, 1930), 42.

5. Hearn, "The Scenes of Cable's Romances," in *An American Miscellany,* II, 168.

Hearn lived in New Orleans until 1887, working for the New Orleans *Item* and later for the *Times-Democrat*. Here both his personal and literary horizons expanded. He made friends with George Washington Cable and with locally prominent men such as Dr. Rudolph Matas, who served as a model for some of Hearn's Creole characters. He continued his translations, began writing editorials and book reviews, and at last had time to read in a variety of subjects that interested him, such as musical theory and mythology. Most important, he began his first original work. Encouraged perhaps by what he considered the sensuous and dreamy aspects of New Orleans, Hearn wrote "fantastics"—short pieces that took real things, kites or kittens, then embellished and projected them into a fantasy world of daydreams and impressions. From his reading he gathered material for his Chinese tales, which he polished and collected in *Some Chinese Ghosts*. [6] Both types of writing reflect his developing fascination with the exotic.

He reworked the Creole sketches which were published in the New Orleans papers into pieces for national publication in *Harper's*. In addition, he contributed to several books about New Orleans which were published in 1885 during the New Orleans Exposition; these were the *Historical Sketch Book and Guide to New Orleans and Environs*, a cookbook, *La Cuisine Creole*, which was entirely his own, and *Gombo Zhèbes: A Little Dictionary of Creole Proverbs*, written two years earlier. [7] A trip to Grand Isle produced enough impressions for *Chita*,

6. Hearn's "fantastics" are collected in *Fantastics and Other Fancies*, ed. Charles Woodward Hutson (Boston: Houghton Mifflin, 1914). *Some Chinese Ghosts* (Boston: Roberts Brothers) appeared in 1887. *Stray Leaves from Strange Literature* (Boston: James R. Osgood), reflecting Hearn's diverse reading, was published in 1884.

7. Lafcadio Hearn, *La Cuisine Creole: A Collection of Culinary Recipes from Leading Chefs and Noted Creole Housewives, Who Have Made New Orleans Famous for Its Cuisine* (New York: Will H. Coleman, 1885). Hearn, *Gombo Zhèbes or Little Dictionary of Creole Proverbs* (New York: Will H. Coleman, 1885); Hearn, *Historical Sketch Book and Guide to New Orleans and Environs* (New York: Will H. Coleman, 1885).

which Hearn completed before leaving for the West Indies. By the end of his New Orleans years he had achieved some national recognition and had realized to some degree his potential for writing.

It is this period of Hearn's life, together with the two years spent in the French West Indies, that is most important to the present study—for though, strictly speaking, the West Indian experience is not part of the southern years, it represents a kind of logical extension of what Hearn found most compelling about Louisiana and its ways. If not part of the southern United States, it was part of Hearn's South. On his first visit to the West Indies he was so enchanted with the island (which represented, he said, a younger, fresher New Orleans) that this brief visit was followed by a two-year sojourn which gave him material for many sketches and a novelette, *Youma.* [8] He made short trips to New York and Philadelphia, but in 1890, still in search of the strange and exotic, he left the United States for Japan. What he found there was not what he had expected, but it bound him for the remainder of his life. His Eastern sketches and tales had foreshadowed his interest in this part of the world, but instead of producing the culmination of his cultivation of the exotic, life in quiet, orderly Japan brought a respected career as a university professor and marriage to a Japanese woman who gave him four children and a feeling of security he had never before experienced. At the conclusion of his life Hearn expressed more contentment with his situation than ever before, but felt that in spite of his numerous writings about Japan he had sacrificed his art for these satisfactions. Elizabeth Bisland,

---

8. Lafcadio Hearn, *Youma: The Story of a West-Indian Slave* (New York: Harper and Brothers, 1890); Hearn, *Two Years in the French West Indies* (New York: Harper and Brothers, 1890).

his friend and later his biographer, wrote: "Despite his disappointments he remained always, to the end of his life, convinced that this world of sun and color was his true *milieu*. 'Ah!
the tropics—' he lamented, long years after, 'they still pull at my
heartstrings... my real field was there.'" [9]

Hearn's search for his own "field for fiction" had its first
success in New Orleans, gateway to the tropical South. Drawing on the South for material was, of course, nothing new,
and Hearn's early use of the material he found there was not
unlike that of other writers. An article in *Harper's* entitled
"The Recent Movement in Southern Literature," discusses
Hearn along with local color writers such as Grace King and
Thomas Nelson Page. [10] His early southern writing justifies
this classification, for although his style could never be confused with that of local color fiction such as Constance Fenimore Woolson's, for example, the two writers shared a deep
admiration for the beauty of the South, unfettered by political
and moral concerns. In his little vignettes of Creole life in
New Orleans and his sketches of the city's picturesque aspects,
Hearn, like the local color writers, records his first impressions
of the differences that made an area unique:

Christmas Eve came in with a blaze of orange glory in the west, and
masses of lemon-colored clouds piled up above the sunset. The
whole city was filled with orange-colored light, just before the sun
went down; and between the lemon-hued clouds and the blue were
faint tints of green. The colors of that sunset seemed a fairy mockery
of the colors of the fruit booths throughout the city; here the golden
fruit lay piled up in luxuriant heaps, and here the awnings of white
canvas had been replaced by long archways of interwoven orange
branches with the fruit still glowing upon them. Walking under

9. Elizabeth Bisland, ed., "Some Martinique Letters of Lafcadio Hearn," *Harper's*,
CXLII (March, 1921), 516–25.
10. Charles W. Coleman, Jr., "The Recent Movement in Southern Literature,"
Harper's, LXXIV (May, 1887), 837–55.

these Christmas booths seemed like walking through a natural bower of heavily freighted fruit trees. It was an Orange Christmas. [11]

This account of Christmas in New Orleans, which Hearn wrote in his early years in the city, suggests the local colorist's preoccupation with qualities that contrast with the ordinary world and, at the same time, hints at the sensitivity of Hearn's perception, which would ultimately develop into greater art than the local color medium offered.

In a sketch written, Hearn records, "principally to offer *Harper's* . . . a totally novel subject of artistic study," he pictures Saint Malo, an isolated village less than a hundred miles from New Orleans but virtually unheard of: "Out of the shuddering reeds and banneretted grass on either side rise the fantastic houses of the Malay fishermen, poised upon slender supports above the marsh, like cranes or bitterns watching for scaly prey. Hard by the slimy mouth of the bayou extends a strange wharf, as ruined and rotted and unearthly as the timbers of the spectral ship in the *Rime of the Ancient Mariner.*" [12] His description here, too, has the detailed setting of local color writing even as it reveals his preoccupation with the strange and exotic.

Another characteristic Hearn shared with Woolson was the view of the Reconstruction era in the South as a period of failure. Thus, in one of his Creole sketches he depicts a visit by the Devil:

The Devil had not been in New Orleans since the period of Reconstruction—a period at which, our readers may remember, it was proverbially said that New Orleans was "going to the Devil."

11. Lafcadio Hearn, "An Orange Christmas" (New Orleans: Paul Veith, 1914). These writings, preserved by Professor "John" Dimitry and a lady relative, were printed for Christmas and distributed "to friends and people who hold Hearn in high esteem." The edition was limited to 150 copies, including one in the Lafcadio Hearn Collection, Tulane University, New Orleans.
12. Hearn, "Saint Malo," in *An American Miscellany*, II, 92.

Such also appears to have been the Devil's own personal opinion. He found things in such a condition about that time that he had not been able to find room in his voluminous breast-pockets for all the mortgages which he had obtained upon men's souls; and believing, from the mad career of Radicalism, that the whole city must be made over to him in the course of a few years, he had departed elsewhere in search of employment. "They have no need of me," said the Devil, "in the State of Louisiana." [13]

Significantly, in this sketch the Devil finds it necessary to return to New Orleans upon hearing of the overthrow of radicalism, implying that a return of control to those formerly in power is a threat to the Devil and consequently a good thing. In this opinion Hearn reflects the sentiments of Woolson, who also sympathized with the white southern desire for self-rule.

Like De Forest, Tourgée, and Woolson, Hearn wrote about the people he encountered in the South, but for him the importance of individuals in their own right is greater. His southerners are neither reduced to foils or backdrops for northerners nor used to illustrate a point. The author's concern with their human qualities distinguishes his writings from the works previously discussed, where even when characters are more extensively developed they are usually exploited for thematic purposes. Hearn, for example, explores the life of a black voudoo purely for the interest it generates in itself, and in his sketch of a Creole servant girl he depicts the mysterious ways of the Negroes who lived closely with whites but whose private thoughts remained always a mystery to their masters. [14]

13. Lafcadio Hearn, "A Visit to New Orleans," in *Leaves from the Diary of an Impressionist; Creole Sketches and Some Chinese Ghosts* (Boston: Houghton Mifflin, 1923), 124, Vol I of *The Writings of Lafcadio Hearn* (16 vols.; Boston: Houghton Mifflin, 1923). Further references to Hearn's collected writings will be to this edition, hereinafter cited as *Writings*.

14. Hearn, "The Last of the Voudoos," in *An American Miscellany*, II, 201–208; and Hearn, "Creole Servant Girls," *Writings*, I, 188–90.

To a much greater degree than the other writers Hearn
sought to present black men in their own milieu, as a valuable
source of literary material in their own right. The sketch "Les
Porteuses" included in *Two Years in the French West Indies*
carefully and lovingly describes the girls who carry merchan-
dise on their heads and thus serve as a major means of commerce in islands such as Martinique.[15] The opening chapter of
Youma describes the "da" who served as foster-mother and
nurse to Creole children and stayed with the child more than
did the real mother: "She alone satisfied all his little needs; he
found her more indulgent, more patient, perhaps even more
caressing, than the other."[16] In *Youma* Hearn's portrayal of
the "da" is such that the girl achieves heroic stature when she
gives her life for her Creole charge. "Her special type was a
product of slavery, largely created by selection: the one creation of slavery perhaps not unworthy of regret—one strange
flowering amid all the rank dark growths of that bitter soil."[17]
Hearn's treatment of this special sort of Negro, the Creole
servant, achieves a reality that goes beyond the stereotype.

The same is true with his other characters. In his sketches
treating the Creole working class he does not criticize them as
society's failures; instead they have color and life and diver-
sity. He saw humor and even virtue in the situation of four
Creole carpenters taking three weeks to put up an awning at a
corner grocery when "two stout Irishmen would have done it
in twenty-four hours." After all, "they did not propose to work
themselves to death. Life was too short."[18] The inhabitants of
the fishing villages in the bayous, earning a meager existence

15. Hearn, "Les Porteuses," in *Two Years in the French West Indies*, Vol. III of
Writings, 115–40.
16. Hearn, in *Two Years in the French West Indies, II: Chita and Youma*, Vol. IV of
Writings, 261–62.
17. *Ibid.*, 263.
18. Hearn, *Leaves from the Diary*, 149.

from the sea, also gained his admiration and he was concerned with presenting accurate pictures of them. For his portrayal of Silvio and Carmen Viosca in *Chita* he drew upon friends for help in recreating the Spanish dialect and patois spoken at Viosca point.

Of the many nationalities represented along the coast, the Basques most fascinated Hearn and stimulated his romantic notions of what he considered to be primitive people. Of a young Basque girl, an inhabitant of a remote fishing village, he wrote: "The strangeness of her beauty is the type of a forgotten people,—that savage and elastic grace an inheritance bequeathed through epochs whose story is written only in Nature's chronicles of stone. . . . I can discern a vague and elegant Something that irresistibly recalls to me one of the most singular chapters in the romance of science,—the osteology of the primitive race."[19] The Basques became for Hearn a living symbol of a younger, fresher world.

Hearn also had great admiration for the aristocratic classes—in New Orleans represented for him by the Creole inhabitants of the French Quarter—those people who Cable said never forgave a public mention. He wrote a number of sketches in which he pictured the secluded life of the old families living in the Quarter. "A Creole Courtyard," describing the contrast between the simple exterior and the richness within, serves as a metaphor for the lives of these people who lived gracefully and quietly, hidden from the glare of the American section of the city:

An atmosphere of tranquility and quiet happiness seemed to envelop the old house, which had formerly belonged to a rich planter. Like many of the Creole houses, the façade presented a commonplace

19. Hearn, "Torn Letters," appendix to *Chita: A Memory of Last Island* (Chapel Hill: University of North Carolina Press, 1969), 209–10.

and unattractive aspect.... But beyond the gates lay a little paradise.... Without, cottonfloats might rumble, and street-cars vulgarly jingle their bells; but these were mere echoes of the harsh outer world which disturbed not the delicious quiet within—where sat, in old-fashioned chairs, good old-fashioned people who spoke the tongue of other times, and observed many quaint and knightly courtesies, forgotten in this material era. Without, roared the Iron Age, the angry waves of American traffic; within, one heard only the murmur of the languid fountain.[20]

The Creoles of Hearn's sketches share the qualities hinted at by De Forest and Tourgée and lavishly praised by Woolson: dignity, grace, refinement, and above all, an adherence to noble old ways that set them apart from the rest of the world.

Although the idealized aspect of the South was presented in the works of the other writers in their depiction of the noble classes, only Hearn seems to have been fully aware of the appeal of this idealization. This is even apparent in a passage written in 1878, just after his arrival in New Orleans. He speaks of the decay of the city "in the midst of the ruined paradise of Louisiana" and surmises that someday a new social system will arise and new prosperity will flourish:

But the new South shall never be as the old. Those once grand residences that are being devoured by mossy decay can never be rebuilt; the old plantation which extended over whole parishes will be parcelled out to a hundred farmers from states that are not Southern; and the foreign beauties of New Orleans will never be restored. It is the picturesqueness of the South, the poetry, the traditions, the legends, the superstitions, the quaint faiths, the family prides, the luxuriousness, the splendid indolence and the splendid sins of the old social system which has passed, or which is now passing away forever. It is all this which is dead or is now dying in New Orleans, and which can hope for no triumphant call to resurrection. The new South may, perhaps, become far richer than the old South; but there will be no aristocracy, no lives of unbridalled luxury, no reckless

20. Hearn, *Leaves from the Diary*, 147–48.

splendors of hospitality, no mad pursuit of costliest pleasure. The old Southern hospitality has been starved to death, and leaves no trace of its former being save the thin ghost of a romance.[21]

And later in a sketch entitled "The Garden of Paradise," appearing in the *Times-Democrat* for March 27, 1883, Hearn reiterates the paradisial aspect of Louisiana, made even more alluring by the fact that it is elusive, never to be completely possessed.

And the great dreaminess of the land makes itself master of thought and speech,—mesmerizes you,—caresses with tender treachery,—soothes with irresistible languor,—woos with unutterable sweetness.... Afterward when you have returned into the vast metropolis, into the dust and the turmoil and the roar of traffic and the smoke of industry and the iron cares of life,—that mesmerism will not have utterly passed away, nor the perfume of that poppied land wholly evaporated from the brain. The songs of the birds will still be heard by you—faint as fairy flutes, and in dreams the golden Teche will curve for you once more under wondrous festoons of green, under wizard apparelled groves, through deep enchantments of perennial summer; and you will awake to feel the great sweet dreaminess come back upon you again—a moment only, but a moment that makes dim the eyes as with mists of a tropical morning.[22]

Not only does Hearn indicate a greater awareness of the fascination of the South, but his liberation from restrictions on how to deal with it enabled him to pursue his interests in directions not open to the other writers. For Hearn the literary evocation of the South was an end in itself. In writing about southern people, lifestyles, and ideals, he directed his energies toward the development of a style which, he felt, was in harmony with his subject matter. Both in his articles for New Orleans newspapers in which he examined the style of contemporary writers and in the letters to friends in which many

21. Hearn, "Orange Christmas," 12.
22. Hearn, "The Garden of Paradise," in *An American Miscellany*, II, 105–106.

of his own attitudes toward style were formulated, there is evident a much greater concern with style than Tourgeé, De Forest, or Woolson showed. His translations and critical re- views reveal some of his prejudices—an admiration for characteristics of impressionism, such as concern with color and the relationship between the receptor and the shapes and forms of the material conveyed by a work, and a dislike for some of the tenets of naturalism. The latter he expressed in a letter to his musicologist friend, H. E. Krehbiel: "But as the copy of Nature is not true art according to the Greek law of beauty, so I believe that the school of Naturalism belongs to the low order of literary creation." [23]

In a later letter to Krehbiel he elaborated on his own theory of style, showing the influence of nineteenth-century roman- ticism in which form and content are organically unified. He refers to his theory as "my ancient dream of a poetical prose—compositions to satisfy an old Greek ear—like chants wrought in a huge measure, wider than the widest line of a Sanscrit composition, and just a little irregular, like Ocean- rhythm. . . . I fancy that I shall have produced a pleasant effect on the reader's mind, simply with pictures; and that the secret work, the word-work, will not be noticed for its own sake." [24] His concern was with the presentation of visual and sensual imagery.

Hearn felt that the conventional novel form would be an inappropriate vehicle for this sort of writing and predicted that the great novel would fade away: "Three-quarters of what is written is unnecessary—is involved simply by obedience to effete formulas and standards. As a consequence we do not read as we used to. We read only the essential, skipping all

23. Lafcadio Hearn to H. E. Krehbiel, 1881, in Elizabeth Bisland (ed.), *Life and Letters of Lafcadio Hearn,* Vol. XIII of *Writings,* 219.
24. Hearn to Krehbiel, October, 1886, *ibid.,* 376.

else. The book that compels perusal of every line and word is
the book of power. Create a story of which no reader can skip
a single paragraph, and one has the secret of force—if not of
durability. My own hope is to do something in accordance
with this idea. . . . nothing but the feeling itself at highest
intensity."[25] Hearn's expressed conviction that the picture
and the feeling it conveyed are most important perhaps explains the two prevailing characteristics of his works that further distinguish them from the other writers. These are the
prevalence of sensual, especially visual, imagery and the absence of moral commentary. In a letter written to his friend
Dr. George M. Gould Hearn indicated that he felt little conflict between morality and the senses: "I suspect what we term
the finer moral susceptibilities signify merely a more complex
and perfect evolution of purely physical sensitiveness. . . .
When one's physical sensibilities are fully developed and
properly balanced, I do not think wickedness to others possible."[26]

Hearn also shared with Gould much of his interest in a
particular refinement of the sensibilities, that of heightened
visual perception. Gould was coauthor of a pamphlet on
"Colour-Sense" which apparently expressed ideas shared by
Hearn.[27] In a letter thanking Gould for the pamphlet he
commented on his own novelette, *Chita*, "When you read the
first part . . . I think you will find much of what you have said
regarding the aesthetic Symbolism of Colour therein expressed, intuitively—especially regarding the holiness of the
sky-colour—the divinity of Blue. Blue is the World-Soul."[28]

25. Hearn to Elizabeth Bisland, 1889, in Elizabeth Bisland (ed.), *Life and Letters of Lafcadio Hearn*, Vol. XIV of *Writings*, 81.
26. Hearn to George M. Gould, October, 1888, *ibid.*, 60.
27. George M. Gould, "Human Colour Sense Considered" (N.p., 1886). A copy of the pamphlet may be found in the Library Company of Philadelphia.
28. Hearn to Gould, April, 1887, in *Letters*, 17–18.

These distinctions—an impressionistic style that placed content above thesis in importance paralleled by an intensity of sensual perception and an absence of moral commentary (Hearn could even lament the passing of a social system that produced octoroons as a gain for morality but a loss for art)— represent key differences between Hearn's southern writings and those of De Forest, Tourgée, and Woolson. But although he developed a unique style, he also developed most fully the portrayal shared by the others of the South as an idealized place.

That Hearn, for example, viewed the color blue as divine reinforces the proposition that his journey to the South was a quest after an ideal world. Often in his letters and sketches he mentioned that blue and other bright colors of this area were always in contrast with the cold, gray North, and his sketches of Louisiana and Florida contain references to tropical blues. Probably the best known of his compositions on blue, however, appears in the opening of his series of sketches "A Midsummer Trip to the Tropics." As a steamer leaves New York the morning is gray until the haze dissolves revealing "a beautiful, pale, vapory, blue—a spiritualized Northern blue." Both sky and sea share this tint. By the second day the sea is "like violet ink" and the sky is "still pale blue." As the steamer glides southward Hearn traces its course by the changing, deepening blue of the sea and sky. When they enter tropic waters "the sea is a flaming, dazzling lazulite." And the author concludes: "All this sensuous blending of warmth and force in winds and waters more and more suggests an idea of the spiritualism of elements—a sense of world-life." [29]

It appears, then, that in contrast to the other writers Hearn

29. Hearn, *Two Years in the French West Indies,* Vol. III of *Writings,* 3, 4, 6, 7, 10, 11.

shows an acute awareness that the South as a source of literary material was especially important because it contained elements that lent themselves to the development of an ideal. Further, because Hearn's major concern was with the presentation or evocation of the material itself, the style he found most appropriate reduced the writer to the role of mere observer. The sketches in *Two Years in the French West Indies,* which begin with description and then intensify until the reader shares with the narrator his feelings of wonder and awe, show the effects of the author's method. Another example of this approach is found in Hearn's best-known American work, *Chita.*

This novelette, recounting the destruction of Last Isle and the fate of two of its survivors, may be seen as the culmination of Hearn's concern with the exotic, of blending form with content. Hearn had experimented with this form in earlier, shorter works such as "The Post Office" and "Torn Letters," which have been cited as forestudies. In his introduction to *Chita* Arlin Turner refers to them as "highly impressionistic, romantic in flavor, and consciously directed toward uniqueness of matter and conception." [30] This statement may also be applied to *Chita,* for although the author here attempts a more elaborate plot, it is largely subordinated to the descriptions, fragmented from the photographic into impressions of the color and shape of the Louisiana Gulf Coast and New Orleans.

Hearn uses the techniques of impressionism, stressing the effect of the material upon its receptor, to evoke from the subject that intensity of feeling he often stated was the goal of this writing. Thus, the seven sections in the first part of the novel, "The Legend of L'Ile Derniere," each repeat a pattern of heightening the effect of description at the conclusion. An

30. Arlin Turner's introduction in Hearn, *Chita,* xix.

account of swimming in the Gulf concludes, "One can aban-
don one's self, without fear of the invisible, to the long, quiv-
ering, electrical caresses of the sea."[31]

In contrast to the previously examined novels there is in
Chita little stress upon self-determination; the focus is on an
account of things simply happening to people, of people swept
along by forces greater than themselves. Thus, the characters
must make only a few moral choices—notably the choice of
Julien La Brierre not to commit suicide; and Hearn deem-
phasizes this by remarking that whether a man lives or dies is
of little consequence to society. The simple elements of
plot—the storm that sweeps away the vacationers at Last Isle,
the rescue of a small girl by a fisherman, and a final meeting
between father and daughter—are events that are not planned
by the characters but simply happen to them.

The dwindling away of plot allows more room for what
Hearn considered more important—the presentation of the
locale and the people, heightened by the use of symbolism.
The first apparent symbol, that of the steamer compared to a
white bird, sets up a predominant thesis of the close relationship between man and nature. The little steamers one catches
at New Orleans to travel to the islands "rest their white
breasts against the levée, side by side—like great weary swans"
(C, [3]–4). The same sort of imagery is apparent in the oaks
on Grand Isle which bend away from the sea "like fleeing
women with streaming garments and wind-blown hair,—
bowing grievously and thrusting out arms desperately north-
ward as to save themselves from falling" (C, 14–15). In both
cases Hearn's thesis—that man and nature are essentially
inseparable—is sustained.

Another major symbol for Hearn is the sea, which represents

31. Hearn, *Chita*, 27. Hereinafter, references to this work will be cited parenthetically in the text.

an abyss, an ambiguous mixture of good and evil, source both of life and destruction of life. This mixture of beauty and horror is most evident in Part One where the gaiety of the dance held in the hotel at Last Isle is paralleled and mocked by the sea: "'*The Wind waltzes to-night, with the Sea for his partner!*' . . . O the stupendous Valse-Tourbillion! O the mighty Dancer! One-two-three! From northeast to east, from east to southeast, from southeast to south: then from the south he came, whirling the Sea in his arms" (C, 48).

Later this same sea, which takes the lives of hundreds including Chita's mother, is for Chita "something that had become tame for her sake, something that loved her in a huge rough way; a tremendous playmate, whom she no longer feared to see come bounding and barking to lick her feet. And little by little, she also learned the wonderful healing and caressing power of the monster, whose cool embrace at once dispelled all drowsiness, feverishness, weariness" (C, 160–61). The sea is not inherently evil; only when man fails to heed its warnings, refuses to acknowledge his proper relationship to nature, is the sea harmful to man.

Although the sea is the strongest single symbol, other aspects of nature also become symbolic. As elsewhere in Hearn's work the colors of sea and sky are dominant throughout. In contrast to the North where "rarely, in the paler zones, do earth and heaven take such luminosity," a summer day on the islands becomes "a caress of color . . . a spirituality, as of eternal tropical spring. It must have been to even such a sky that Xenophanes lifted up his eyes of old when he vowed the Infinite Blue was God" (C, 20).

In a sense, the symbolism of sea, sky, and color are inseparable. They merge and blend together, the changes of one reflecting the shifting of another. And this connection reflects a unity of meaning, for the natural elements and their colors represent for Hearn the beauty and divinity sought by all men: "Ever, as the sun floats higher, the flood shifts its color. Sometimes smooth and gray, yet flickering with the morning gold, it is the vision of John,—the apocalyptic Sea of Glass mixed with fire. . . . Once more, under the blaze of noon, it changes to a waste of broken emerald. With evening, the horizon assumes tints of inexpressible sweetness,—pearl-lights, opaline colors of milk and fire. . . . Then, if the sea sleeps, it dreams of all these,—faintly, weirdly,—shadowing them even to the verge of heaven" (C, 22-23).

Blues and greens, the colors of nature, permeate the book, and only when the author wishes to show death, man's final loss of the paradise of nature, do other colors predominate. When, at the conclusion of the novel, Julien loses his battle with tropical fever, the room is "filled with ruby-colored light." The sky becomes "Red—black-red," and then, as death approaches, it becomes "black, starless" (C, 202, 204).

The key to the premise that Hearn is presenting an idealized place in *Chita* is the predominance of the color blue. Further, the novel contains two variations of this ideal. First, there is the passing grandeur represented by Last (constantly evoking "lost") Isle, the destruction of the gentle, noble Creoles being a metaphor for the passing of the old order in the South. And those who do survive, like Julien, find that nothing will ever be the same. When he returns to New Orleans there is no place for him in society, and Hearn comments on Julien's action in taking up as a profession the medicine he had studied only as an accomplishment: "After the passing of that huge shock, which left all the imposing and splendid fabric of Southern feudalism wrecked forever, his profession stood him in good stead" (C, 170).

But in place of the ideal evoked by the other writers—of the days of splendor and chivalry—Hearn suggests the beauty of tropical nature. The transition from one to the other is embodied in the metamorphosis of Chita (formerly Zouzoune) from small, elegant Creole to a child of nature. In Part Three, in an extended evaluation of Chita's situation, the narrator asks: "What had she lost of life by her swift translation from the dusty existence of cities to the open immensity of nature's freedom? What did she gain?" She lost "those little bitternesses and restraints and disappointments which all well-bred city children must suffer in the course of their training for the more or less factitious life of society" (C, 147). Instead, "she saw and heard and felt much of that which, though old as the heavens and the earth, is yet eternally new and eternally young with the holiness of beauty,—eternally mystical and divine,—eternally weird: the unveiled magnificence of Nature's moods,—the perpetual poem hymned by wind and surge,—the everlasting splendor of the sky" (C, 148–49).

Although Hearn shifts the focus of his ideal, or rather intensifies it until it becomes merged with the physicality of the South itself, it shares a common characteristic with the other novels—a sense of the elusive past. Hearn describes the Louisiana coast where Chita is saved as having an "aspect . . . not of the present, but of the immemorial past—of that epoch when low flat reaches of primordial continent first rose into form above a Silurian Sea" (C, 63). And Silvio and Carmen Viosca, who become Chita's new parents, are themselves remnants of a simple life more prevalent in bygone days. Hearn reminds us that the life of the bayous is constantly threatened by encroaching civilization.

For Hearn, however, there was in nature some measure of chance for stability. In the divine blue of the sea and sky he found hope of a lasting paradise. Consequently, in *Chita* the lives of the main characters remain always subordinate to the forces of nature, and in the face of the power and greatness of

the tropical surroundings man's actions are displaced in importance. For Hearn the importance of man is as a receiver of
impressions, not as a judge. His reason for writing such a novel
was to reflect and mirror the beauty revealed to man, to blend
form and content in projecting the intensity of feeling evoked
by the splendor of the South.

It has been suggested, with justification, that *Chita* is a
flawed work, that Parts Two and Three fail to meet the prom-
ise of the opening section. Hearn attempts too much in the
third part when he compresses ten years of Chita's life into a
brief section.[32] This section fails to make clear why Julien is
reunited with his daughter only to die, and the conclusion is
perhaps weakened by shifting the point of view to Julien with
little apparent artistic justification. But if *Chita* ultimately
fails, it is perhaps because Hearn violates his own principle of
dealing with only a single theme and paring away all that is
not necessary. For this reason Part One is the novel's best
part. In the picture of the Gulf Coast, the description of the
confrontation between man and nature and the struggle
among natural forces, Hearn achieved his dream of a poetical
prose, of word pictures as poetical jewels. "Forever the yellow
Mississippi strives to build; forever the sea struggles to
destroy;—and amid their eternal strife the islands and the
promontories change shape, more slowly, but not less fantas-
tically, than the clouds of heaven" (C, 15).

Hearn wrote later that he was unhappy with *Chita*, but as
Lewis Leary notes, "He could not have been thinking of the
first section, which is heightened surely, but which in tone
and substance is almost exactly right." Leary ranks the first

32. Lewis Leary, "Lafcadio Hearn, 'One of our Southern Writers': A Footnote to
Southern Literary History," in Clarence Gohdes (ed.), *Essays on American Literature
in Honor of Jay B. Hubbell* (Durham: Duke University Press, 1967), 213.

part of *Chita* with Mark Twain's "Old Times on the Mississippi," which Hearn admired, and Thoreau's accounts of Katahdin and Cape Cod.[33] If Leary's is an accurate assessment, then of the writers examined thus far it was Hearn who achieved the greatest success in writing about the South for the purpose of creating art in language.

33. *Ibid.*

V

Owen Wister and the Southern Rebuke

A player in a word association game, being given the name Owen Wister, would (if he recognized the name at all) quickly respond "the Virginian" or "Wild West" or simply "cowboy." Each of these would be appropriate answers, for Wister's fame as a novelist rests firmly upon his popularization, even idealization, in *The Virginian* of the rugged, manly cowboy who became a national idol.[1]

But in addition to his numerous writings of the western frontier, Owen Wister also wrote about the South, and our player might just have correctly answered "old Charleston," "the aristocratic South," or "*Lady Baltimore.*"[2] And it is with these seemingly unrelated themes—America's frontier heritage and the bygone gentility of the old South—that Wister may be drawn into our circle of writers who explored alternatives to the urban, industrialized lifestyle which has increasingly characterized this nation from the post-Civil War era to the present.

G. Edward White, in *The Eastern Establishment and the Western Experience*, has carefully traced the causes, conditions, and results of Owen Wister's perennial migrations to

1. Owen Wister, *The Virginian* (New York: Macmillan, 1902). Hereinafter, references to this work will be cited parenthetically in the text.
2. Owen Wister, *Lady Baltimore* (1905; Ridgewood, N.J.: Gregg Press, 1968). Hereinafter, references to this work will be cited parenthetically in the text.

the West. Wister, as well as his friends and contemporaries Theodore Roosevelt and the illustrator, Frederic Remington, came to terms with the differences resulting from the polarities inherent in nineteenth-century America. These contrasts pitted urban life, big business, and the multi-ethnic backgrounds characteristic of the East against their opposites, the images of a rural, individualistic, and ethnically homogeneous West.[3] White sees the aim of these men as one of reasserting a "rural, egalitarian, Anglo-Saxon heritage"—of attempting to create an agrarian-based utopia to take the place of urban industrial society.[4] He does not extend his "utopia" thesis to Wister's treatment of the South in his fiction, but a relationship can be established.

Wister's western experience could not have been predicted. The grandson of the famous Shakespearean actress, Fanny Kemble, Wister grew up in Philadelphia, the only son of a prosperous businessman and his intellectual wife. He attended private schools in Europe as well as at Groton and Harvard, where he formed a friendship with upperclassman Theodore Roosevelt which would become stronger as the two men indulged their mutual fondness for the western frontier. As a youth Wister wanted to become a composer and studied in Europe where he was praised by Franz Liszt as having "un talent prononcé." He was approaching a decision to devote himself to music when his father secured for him an excellent position in a brokerage firm and called him home to a career in business. The position did not materialize, however, and Wister found himself relegated to being a clerk in the firm.

In 1885, probably as a partial result of his thwarted career

---

3. G. Edward White, *The Eastern Establishment and the Western Experience: The West of Frederic Remington, Theodore Roosevelt, and Owen Wister* (New Haven: Yale University Press, 1968), [147].

4. *Ibid.*, 185.

hopes and his entrapment in a tedious job, Wister's health broke down and he went to Wyoming as a cure. He remarked of the trip, "This accidental sight of the cattle-country settled my career."[5] Although he did return East to study law and, after joining the bar in 1888, to settle into a Philadelphia law firm, his heart remained in the West. The journey to Wyoming was the first of numerous annual visits westward, and the time spent in the law office was usually employed in germinating ideas for his western fiction.

An oft-repeated anecdote told by Wister concerns his decision to capture the West in fiction. By 1891 he had spent five summers in Wyoming and kept a diary of his experiences which he termed "faithful, realistic."[6] Back East in the autumn of 1891 he dined with friends and the question arose, "Why wasn't some Kipling saving the sage-brush for American literature, before the sage-brush and all that it signified went the way of the California forty-niner, went the way of the Mississippi steam-boat, went the way of everything? Roosevelt had seen the sage-brush true, had felt its poetry; and also Remington, who illustrated his articles so well. But what was fiction doing, fiction, the only thing that has always outlived fact?"[7] Wister reports that he decided on impulse to "save the sage-brush," and, as he recounted it, "I went up to the library; and by midnight or so, a good slice of *Hank's Woman* was down in the rough. I followed it soon with *How Lin McLean Went East*. Lin was my camp companion in *Hank's Woman*."[8] Both stories were published in 1892.[9]

5. Owen Wister, *Roosevelt: The Story of a Friendship, 1880–1919* (New York: Macmillan, 1930), 28.
6. *Ibid.*
7. *Ibid.*, 29.
8. *Ibid.*
9. Owen Wister, "Hank's Woman," *Harper's Weekly*, XXXVI (August 27, 1892),

The Virginian, upon which Wister's fame was made, was written between 1891 and 1902. Episodes already published in magazine form comprised about half the book when Wister collected and structured them into the novel published in 1902.[10] Wister commented that he had substituted the cowboy known only as the Virginian or the Southerner for his previously successful Lin McLean because he felt he "needed a 'Greek chorus' of an intelligence more subtle than Lin's."[11]

This transfer of emphasis from the simple, vernacular Lin to the more complex Virginian has been commented on by Neal Lambert, who feels that the early story, "How Lin McLean Went East," clearly affirms an essentially vernacular West while negating the genteel East.[12] Here Wister portrayed a cowboy who returns to his childhood home in Massachusetts only to recognize the irreconcilable differences between himself and his city-bred brother. His brother has achieved some small stature through his membership in a club "where the paying-tellers of banks played cards every night, and the head clerk at the Parker House was president."[13] Sensing that his brother is ashamed for his friends to meet Lin in his western clothes, Lin breaks with him and returns to Wyoming. In spurning his brother, Lin realizes that his real family lives not in the East but in the West. It is not this snobbish brother but the cowboys who are his true kin.[14]

"How Lin McLean Went East" is clearly a story in which

821–23; Wister, "How Lin McLean Went East," *Harper's Magazine,* LXXXVI (December, 1892), 135–46.

10. N. Orwin Rush, "Fifty Years of *The Virginian,*" *Papers of the Bibliographical Society of America,* XLVI (1952), 103.

11. Wister, *Roosevelt,* 29.

12. Neal Lambert, "Owen Wister's Lin McLean: The Failure of the Vernacular Hero," *Western American Literature,* V (1970), 220.

13. Wister, "How Lin McLean Went East," 144.

14. Lambert, "Owen Wister's Lin McLean," 221.

Wister explicitly refuted such "false" eastern values as the worship of money and success in business and affirmed the values of freedom and self-autonomy associated with frontier life. But as Wister continued to work with Lin McLean he seemed to realize that his own attitudes were inconsistent with those of his creation. Lambert has compared the Lin of "How Lin McLean Went East" (Dec., 1892) to Lin in *Lin McLean* (1897) to reveal how Wister increasingly added "genteel" touches to the rough-and-tumble cowboy. It is as if Wister found Lin's actions and opinions contrary to much that the author himself valued. From being the man "whom among all cowpunchers I loved most" in "Hank's Woman," Lin had become a problem. To civilize him would have destroyed his essential nature, and Wister was unable to develop Lin's character in another direction.[15]

For this reason, then, Wister chose to develop the Virginian as his "Greek chorus." Although he admired the freedom of the West which the vernacular hero Lin represented, Wister saw that it would not serve as a satisfactory substitute for all his eastern values. In particular, Lin lacked the aristocratic qualities Wister clearly admired—qualities which were absent in the new men of the West and which Wister feared were becoming in short supply in the commercial Northeast. The author did find another and more acceptable alternative through his visits to the South and his idealization of the aristocratic society of old Charleston. But this was to come later, and the character of the Virginian which combined the best that the Lin McLeans of the West could offer, together with the genteel qualities of the East, served as a transitional figure for Wister until he found the culminating formula for his ideal in *Lady Baltimore. The*

15. *Ibid.*, 228.

Virginian thus forms an intermediary step in Wister's search for the ideal counterpoint to an urban, northern lifestyle.

From the opening page of *The Virginian* the author's concern with the East-West dichotomy is evident. Chapter One introduces us to an eastern dude (very much, perhaps, like the young Wister himself) taking his first look at the West through the glass of a Pullman car. From this once-removed perspective, the narrator gets his first look at the Virginian, and the growth of his friendship with the cowboy parallels his increasing initiation into western ways.

Having come from the East to visit the ranch of his friend, Judge Henry, the narrator is met at the railroad station by the tall cowboy known in the novel as the Virginian. In their first meeting it is the easterner who suffers by comparison. Noting that the cowboy has been teasing a grizzled old man who is about to take a bride after numerous unsuccessful attempts, the narrator asks if there are "many oddities out here like Uncle Hughey?" The Virginian smoothly replies, "Yes, seh, there is a right smart of oddities around. They come in on every train" (V, 10). Reflecting on this response, the narrator concludes that it is deserved: "This handsome, ungrammatical son of the soil had set between us the bar of his cold and perfect civility. No polished person could have done it better. . . . If he had tried familiarity with me the first two minutes of our acquaintance, I should have resented it; by what right, then, had I tried it with him? It smacked of patronizing: on this occasion he had come off the better gentleman of the two" (V, 11–12). With this statement the author establishes the dual nature of the Virginian—his affinity with the West coupled with an innate sense of gentility.

These qualities of naturalness and what may be called honor, which are inherent in the Virginian, are developed in the novel alongside the vernacular or western characteristics

that were dominant in Wister's earlier portrayals of the cowboy. The Virginian displays his western prowess and exuberance when he succeeds in getting a bed to himself at a
Medicine Bow boarding house by retiring fully armed after
confiding to his bedmate that he is subject to fits, and in such
incidents as the infamous baby-swapping foray in which he
and Lin McLean swap the clothing of some dozen sleeping
babes while their parents dance at a barbecue. One of Wister's
best accounts of the Virginian's vernacular qualities is a scene
in which he rids Judge Henry and his guests of a hellfire and
brimstone traveling preacher. In this episode the narrator and
the Virginian are sharing quarters with Dr. McBride, the
preacher. Throughout the night the Virginian appears to be
wrestling with the devil—"I'm afeared! I'm afeared! Sin has
quit being bitter in my belly"—and the good doctor wrestles
through the long hours for the cowboy's soul. Only in the
morning, the narrator informs us, does Dr. McBride realize
the trick:

> "You'll be going to breakfast and the ladies, seh, pretty soon," said
> the Virginian, with a chastened voice. "But I'll worry through the
> day somehow without yu'. And to-night you can turn your wolf loose
> on me again."
> Once more it was no use. My face was deep in the pillow, but I
> made sounds as of a hen who has laid an egg. It broke on the Doctor
> with a total instantaneous smash, quite like an egg (V, 245–46).

In these episodes and others the Virginian reflects the natural,
open aspects of frontier life Wister and his fellow easterners
liked to imagine. But to think of Wister's protagonist primarily as a merry prankster would do an injustice to this character's real sense of honor and justice.

The Virginian's gentlemanly qualities and high ethics, although unlike those of easterners, are nevertheless highly refined and obviously considered by Wister as a valid alternative

to those of the urban, Northeast establishment: "The cowpuncher's ungoverned hours did not unman him. If he gave
his word, he kept it; Wall Street would have found him behind the times. Nor did he talk lewdly to women; Newport
would have thought him old-fashioned" (*V*, ix). The reader is
told explicitly that among these men the Virginian is the
cream of the crop: "He was one of thousands drifting and
living thus, but (as you shall learn) one in a thousand" (*V*,
52).

Lambert has noted that in idealizing the Virginian, Wister
was able to bring together in a single character the best qualities of essentially contradictory value systems, the Virginian
being "both frontiersman and gentleman." [16] This statement,
though correct, should be modified slightly to take into account the basic gentlemanly code of honor among cowboys.
This code is evidenced in a number of ways—the refusal to
welch on one's companions as seen in the action of two cattle
rustlers who are hanged, the unwritten rules as to how to treat
one's horse, and the correct demeanor to assume before a lady.
Although the Virginian possesses qualities that link him with
the world east of the frontier, his rigid adherence to the code
of frontier ethics is enough to cause him to be recognized as a
gentleman by his cowpuncher peers. And Wister places great
emphasis on the opinion of the Virginian's sweetheart, Molly
Wood, and his employer, Judge Henry, both easterners who
nevertheless admire the cowboy largely for his adherence to
the frontier code.

In addition, the qualities of the cowboy hero include an
indifference to material gain. Wister poses this indifference,
shared by both the aristocracy and the cowboy, as an alterna-

16. Neal Lambert, "Owen Wister's Virginian: The Genesis of a Cultural Hero,"
Western American Literature, VI (1971), 100.

tive to the money-grubbing activities of the eastern establishment. If the Virginian does acquire wealth (and we learn that
he owns land) it is done casually and not through an active
prostitution of himself to Mammon. [17] Perhaps the Virginian's
comments to the narrator on East-West differences best reflect
Wister's admiration of the western code exemplified by his
hero in this novel: "Now back East you can be middling and
get along. But if you go to try a thing on in this Western
country, you've got to do it *well*" (V, 399). The Virginian has
been speaking of another cowboy who died as a result of his
mediocrity. In Wister's West only the exceptional can survive.

The East-West dichotomy apparent from the outset of *The
Virginian* is nowhere more in evidence than in a major plot
device of the novel—the Virginian's courtship of the schoolteacher Molly Wood. We have seen how such writers as De
Forest, Tourgée, and Woolson employed the North-South
romance motif for various purposes with varying success. To
say that Wister made a hit with his East-West courtship would
be understatement.

The two lovers are pitted as opposites in many ways; Wister
carefully provides background and genealogy for each. Molly
is Vermont born and bred, of a distinguished family descend-
ing from the renowned General Stark. She would have properly "come out" in Bennington society had not the mills failed
that year, plunging the family into genteel poverty. Molly's
decision to go West to teach in the Bear Creek school is
motivated partly by her need to escape a highly acceptable
suitor whom unfortunately (in her family's eyes at least) she
does not love, and to cease being a financial burden on the

17. Mody C. Boatright, "The American Myth Rides the Range: Owen Wister's
Man on Horseback," *Southwest Review,* XXXVI (1951), [157].

already-strained family resources. In her movement West she carries with her her pride in her family—symbolized by a miniature portrait of her Grandmother Stark—and her firm belief in the manners and etiquette in which she has been trained.

The Virginian's move westward is different in a number of ways. He leaves his family not because he fears being a burden to them, but rather because he is disenchanted with these farmers who have no desire to know about a world beyond their restrictive one of crops and hunting. He is not ashamed of his ancestors, but recognizes that there have been no distinguished men among them. Further, having left home at fourteen he has not had a formal education, but rather gained practical knowledge as he drifted from one western territory to another.

Molly's first encounter with the Virginian would seem to give him the advantage—he saves her from a stage stalled at a ford. But he leaves without telling her his name, and at their next meeting—the barbecue at which the baby-swapping occurs—she achieves her advantage over him by refusing to dance with him without being properly introduced. At this point, and during much of the courtship that follows, Molly seems to have the advantage and to assert her superiority over the cowboy. Although we are told that at the dance the Virginian's costume "seemed to radiate romance" to Molly and that she is attracted by his "wildness" and strength, we also learn that she has a number of other admirers and has deep reservations concerning the Virginian's appropriateness as a suitor.

As teacher in the Bear Creek school Molly is superior to her charges; she assumes a similar role in her courtship. The Virginian acknowledges her superiority in education and genteel ways and tells her that he will be her best pupil. The author shows him straining like any schoolboy as he spends a winter with copybooks and primers wearing out one stubby pencil after another practicing handwriting and spelling. Molly also introduces the cowboy to literature, and he is impressed with Shakespeare, although to Molly's disappointment he balks at Jane Austen.

It seems for a while, though, that the cowboy will not meet Molly's standards, and her decision to return to the East is largely influenced by a conversation in which the Virginian appears unwilling to continue as her pupil. She scolds him for returning *Emma* and *Pride and Prejudice* unread: "'Why, it has come too late,' he had told her when the scolding was over. 'If I was one of your little scholars hyeh in Bear Creek school house, yu' could learn me to like such frillery I reckon. But I'm a mighty ignorant growed-up man'" (V, 320). Molly's decision to break the courtship is explained by the author: "No great-aunt at Dunbarton, or anybody else that knew her and her family, should ever say that she had married below her station, had been an unworthy Stark!" (V, 319).

In the end, however, Molly capitulates, and on the Virginian's terms. In a melodramatic touch Wister has Molly discover the cowboy lying near death from an Indian attack. She helps nurse him back to health in her own cabin, where all her belongings stand packed in boxes for the journey East. During the weeks of his convalescence Molly reads *Emma* to him (although it puts him to sleep), and in a crucial love scene the Virginian asks her forgiveness for wasting her time and withdraws his suit. But now that she has been released, it is Molly who asks him to "try to keep me happy!"—to continue the courtship: "Her better birth and schooling that had once been weapons to keep him at his distance, or bring her off victorious in their encounters, had given way before the onset of the natural man himself" (V, 354, 448).

The major capitulation of Molly's eastern values to the frontier ones of the Virginian comes on the eve of their wedding day. The Virginian encounters his old enemy Trampas, a cowpuncher turned cattle rustler who has long resented the Virginian's honesty and innate superiority. Trampas insults the Virginian, making necessary a gun duel in accordance with the frontier code. Although Molly warns him that to fight Trampas is to cancel their wedding plans, the Virginian goes through with it. After the duel, in which Trampas is killed, Molly gives in and the author states, "Thus did her New England conscience battle to the end, and, in the end, capitulate to love" (V, 482).

Near the end of the novel, after the marriage of Molly and the Virginian, Wister makes even more explicit comparisons between West and East. And significantly, the western frontier is here treated with images that may be termed idealized. In an earlier chapter in which the Virginian and the narrator meet in east Idaho the culminating images of the conclusion are foreshadowed: "At noon, when for a while I had thrown off my long oilskin coat, merely the sight of the newspaper half crowded into my pocket had been a displeasing reminder of the railway, and cities, and affairs" (V, 374). A little later the narrator comments, "I was steeped in a revery as of the primal earth" (V, 374). Such images are a clear statement of the easterner's "escape" into the wilderness. But it is on the honeymoon trip of the cowboy and Molly in which they camp on a remote river island that Wister makes his clearest statement of the primal, idealized lure of the West: "So many visits to this island had he made, and counted so many hours of revery spent in its haunting sweetness, that the spot had come to seem his own. It belonged to no man, for it was deep in the unsurveyed and virgin wilderness" (V, 484). The island was so removed from civilization that "the ploughed and planted country, that quilt of many-colored harvests which they had watched yesterday, lay in another world" (V, 486). The Virginian, revealing to Molly the ultimate escapist appeal of the island, says, "Often when I have camped here, it has made me want to become the ground, become the water, become the trees, mix with the whole thing. Not know myself from it" (V, 493). And he thus counterpoints eastern civilization with a West that lures one toward an almost nonhuman unity.

But Wister could not finally reject civilization itself, and so the novel does not stop here. In the final chapter the Virginian and Molly journey East to confront her family, and we see that the hero is no western wildman but can, when he wishes, assume the trappings of eastern gentility. Unlike his predecessor Lin McLean, the Virginian can adapt when necessary to eastern ways—indeed, can outdo these ways, as he does in the scene in which the couple arrive in Bennington. "To see get out of the train merely a tall man with a usual straw hat, and Scotch homespun suit of a rather better cut than most in Bennington—this was dull" (V, 498–99). Further, Molly's great-aunt, long her mentor, implicitly gives her stamp of approval to Molly's husband while speaking of the revered ancestor, General Stark: "New Hampshire was full of fine young men in those days. But nowadays most of them have gone away to seek their fortunes in the West" (V, 501). Thus, the Virginian is accepted by those who count in Molly's world, and there is a seeming reconciliation in him of eastern and western values.

I have suggested earlier that the Virginian serves as a transitional figure for Wister, as gentleman cowboy, as frontiersman tempered with a sense of gentility. In an article on *The Virginian*, Mody Boatright notes that above all a gentleman is chivalrous and that Wister's cowboy embodies the chivalry belonging to an aristocratic South tempered by the frontier West.[18] Thus, he implies what has been overlooked by a number of critics—that the Virginian *is* a Virginian. From the first, Wister commented on this, stating that the cowboy has a "voice . . . Southern and gentle and drawling." In a recital about the villain Trampas, the Virginian slips into southern accent, and "with the light turn he gave it, its pure ugliness melted into charm." This last statement is very similar to one made by Wister in his biography of Roosevelt: "There's a charm about the mere twinkle in a certain sort of Southern eye that goes with their pronunciation and makes you glad the war is all long over."[19]

If the eastern establishment is a place from which one should escape, yet the West, with its lack of tradition and heritage, is not a completely workable alternative to it, the character of the Virginian may be seen as a compromise on the part of the writer—the combination of rugged manliness with an overlay of not eastern, then, but southern chivalric manners. The Virginian, although not a plantation aristocrat, shares with the aristocrat a freedom from money-grubbing and the taint of commercialism, and this serves as a rebuke to the crassness Wister saw encroaching on the eastern establishment. Wister worked on much of *The Virginian* while in Charleston, and the effect of the locale seems to have had at least an indirect effect. The Virginian triumphs as a tempering of the best of the West with that of the South.

Although urged to write a sequel to *The Virginian*, Wister chose instead to follow it with a novel set in the South, and in *Lady Baltimore* he seems to have found the true counterpoint for the shortcomings of the northeastern establishment. Wister stated after the success of *The Virginian*, "Never again can I

18. *Ibid.*, 159.
19. Wister, *Roosevelt*, 40.

light on a character so engaging," but even though he did not wish to write a sequel, he did have the desire to write another book. He felt he needed another setting but would only write about something he knew well. [20] By the time *Lady Baltimore* was written, he did indeed know a good deal about its setting, old Charleston.

Although a true product of the Northeast in background and education, Wister had strong family ties with South Carolina. His great-great grandfather, Major Pierce Butler, had married into the prominent Middleton family of South Carolina and became an illustrious citizen of the state. Many of the Middletons were buried in the cemetery of St. Michael's Church in Charleston, a place that appears often in *Lady Baltimore*. [21] In addition to this direct family connection which allowed him access to some of the leading Charleston families, Wister learned much about the area during his several extended visits there. In addition to traveling through the South on his trips West, he occasionally accompanied his mother on visits to relatives in southern resort areas. In 1898 he and his wife honeymooned in the South, and of their stay in Charleston the groom wrote his mother, "Of all the American towns I've ever come into as a stranger, it's incomparably the most charming." [22] During their stay of almost a month they visited all the major landmarks and enjoyed the hospitality of the best families of Charleston. [23]

They made a second extended visit, from early January until

20. Julian Mason, "Owen Wister: Champion of Old Charleston," *Quarterly Journal of the Library of Congress*, XXIX (1972), 164–65. For a shorter version of this article see Mason, "Owen Wister and the South," *Southern Humanities Review*, VI (1972), 23–34.

21. Mason, "Owen Wister: Champion of Old Charleston," 163.

22. Letter from Owen Wister to his mother, April 24, 1898, quoted in Mason, "Owen Wister: Champion of Old Charleston," 165.

23. Mason, "Owen Wister: Champion of Old Charleston," 165.

spring in 1902, when Mrs. Wister was a commissioner to the Woman's Department of the South Carolina Inter-State and West Indian Exposition. During this period Wister was completing *The Virginian,* which was published in April. It was also at this time that his old friend President Roosevelt paid a three-day official visit to the exposition. Roosevelt was treated cordially, although he was not invited into the homes of Charleston's first families, as had been the Wisters. [24] The relatively good relations between this northern president and Charleston residents were later shattered by what some Charlestonians thought were treasonable actions by Roosevelt, and Wister discussed this incident in both his biography of Roosevelt and *Lady Baltimore.* Of the 1902 visit Wister wrote that perhaps then the germ of *Lady Baltimore* had come into being. "In those months it may well be that this portrait, not yet contemplated, was nevertheless taking on not so much shape as color, all unknown to me, as I pegged away at *The Virginian,* or marvelled at Charleston during Roosevelt's vertiginous visit, or wandered and meditated and looked across the dreamy, empty rivers to their dreamy, empty shores and the gray-veiled live-oaks that were all of a piece with the wistful silence." [25]

A third visit to the South took place in 1905, when for health reasons Wister journeyed to Camden, South Carolina, in January. He was already well along in the writing of *Lady Baltimore,* for he reported to his mother that in Camden he was visited by George Brett of Macmillan Company, to whom he read the novel. During this stay Wister played guide to Henry James in Charleston, a most helpful service to James since Wister was able to secure for him invitations into the

24. *Ibid.,* 165–66.
25. Wister, *Roosevelt,* 103.

homes of the oldest, most prominent families. James's visit, which lasted from February 10 to 13, is described in *The American Scene*. Not surprisingly, what James perceived as important about Charleston corresponds to Wister's observations in *Lady Baltimore*. [26] Wister also read portions of *Lady Baltimore* to James, and it was James who suggested using a name other than Charleston for the setting in order to achieve greater freedom in his treatment of it. James's influence was apparent in other ways as well. In an account of a conversation between the men Wister reportedly confessed that the narrator of *Lady Baltimore* "sounded remarkably" like James. James countered, "Well, my dear Owen, may I in all audacity and sincerity ask, what could Augustus better sound like?" [27] As he completed the novel, Wister also "tried it out" on two Charleston ladies of considerable prominence. Susan Pringle and Harriet Horry Ravenel, the author of works about Charleston, encouraged him and corrected errors. Their influence was so great that Wister once destroyed a chapter that had offended them.

The novel first appeared in shortened form in the *Saturday Evening Post,* from October 28, 1905, to January 27, 1906. Its reception was good among both its northern and southern readers. The book version, published by Macmillan in April, 1906, was a best seller. Fifty thousand copies were sold in two months, and more than ninety thousand copies were sold in the five years following its publication. Although Wister's reputation as the author of *The Virginian* probably helped sales, the success of *Lady Baltimore* was due to its appeal to a large reading audience. Many felt that it would help mend the split between North and South, [28] and Thomas Bailey Aldrich

26. Mason, "Owen Wister: Champion of Old Charleston," 170.
27. *Ibid.,* 172.
28. *Ibid.,* 173, 177.

wrote of the novel, "It's an odd thing that the North should write the South's novel for her!" With a few notable exceptions *Lady Baltimore* was greeted with as much enthusiasm as had been *The Virginian*. [29]

Few critics would disagree that *Lady Baltimore* contained many indictments of the North and was largely a prosouthern novel. The fact that this did not diminish its widespread appeal indicates the changes in attitude about the South which had come full circle by the first decade of the twentieth century. Reconstruction was generally viewed by southerners and most northerners to have been a failure, and only a minority in the North opposed the establishment of Jim Crow laws. Thus, when *Lady Baltimore* espoused the plight of white southerners and the general inferiority of the black man, few of Wister's contemporaries were offended.

Julian Mason has noted that the plot of *Lady Baltimore* seems secondary to other considerations, appearing "more as a thin frame to hold the canvas for a painting of that part of old Charleston still existing in the 20th century than for its own sake, except as the plot provides an opportunity for criticism of those who represent the opposite of old Charleston." [30] Indeed, the predominant quality of the novel appears not in plot or characterization but in the author's explicit comparisons of North and South, in which Charleston (here called Kings Port) is held up as a model for all the positive values that the nation, specifically the Northeast, has forsaken. For in Kings Port the idea that it is blood, not skill in money-

29. Thomas Bailey Aldrich to Hamilton Mabie, June 21, 1906, quoted in Mason, "Owen Wister: Champion of Old Charleston," 180. Two adverse reactions came from Wister's cousin, S. Weir Mitchell of Philadelphia, who wrote Wister, "I am sorry that many people accept as your belief the idea that the south is refined and the north vulgar," and Theodore Roosevelt. See Mason, "Owen Wister: Champion of Old Charleston," 180.

30. Mason, "Owen Wister: Champion of Old Charleston," 175.

getting, that counts is sustained by the old aristocracy who have not yet been completely overrun by the rise of the industrial rich, as had happened in the North.

As in *The Virginian,* the narrator, Augustus, is a northerner (much like Wister himself) who is initiated into a section of the country to which he is a newcomer. In this way the reader is allowed to see the setting through curious and observant eyes. At the same time, the narrator, as a product of life in the North, can speak with authority when contrasting life there with his observations of life in Kings Port. Ostensibly paying a visit to find records proving a royal connection in his ancestral line, Augustus, a young man in his late twenties, becomes more involved with living persons than the dead ancestors his Philadelphia Aunt Carola has directed him to study.

Augustus, like Wister, is given access through letters of introduction to the finest families in Kings Port, and his growing acquaintance with these people is accompanied by an increasing admiration for them, coupled with a disgust for a northern society in which all the old values have been lost. The narrator's comments to this effect are so numerous that they frequently bring the progress of the novel to a standstill. They may be represented by a comment on the cemetery of St. Michael's Church: "There was a total absence of obscure grocers reposing under gigantic obelisks; to earn a monument here you must win a battle, or do, at any rate, something more than adulterate sugar and oil" (*LB*, 58–59).

The narrator repeatedly emphasizes that Kings Port has retained those virtues which the nation, as a whole, has lost. Stating that the genteel, ancient ladies of Kings Port "have made me homesick for a national and a social past which I never saw, but which my old people knew" (*LB*, 65), he concludes that in the past the United States constituted a family, but that all those qualities remaining in Kings Port have been ground into oblivion in the North. Wister stresses that an aristocrat is an aristocrat North or South, that these people have more in common with one another than either does with the sons of toil (except as peasantry) and the vulgar nouveau riche. Yet because the aristocracy of the North has been inundated with the "yellow rich," only in the South are the aristocratic ideals still unadulterated. This is stated most succinctly when Augustus tells a Kings Port native that southern society retains "the manners we've lost, the decencies we've banished, the standards we've lowered, their light is still flickering in this passing generation of yours" (LB, 72-73).

That the narrator sympathizes strongly with the southern attitude toward Reconstruction is evident in his conversation with the young heroine of the novel, Eliza La Heu. When he asks her why the South has not rebuilt the way the United States did after its battle with Britain, she replies, "Did England then set loose on us a pack of black savages and politicians to help us rebuild?" (LB, 201). And the narrator agrees with her sentiments.

It is in the narrator's comments on the southern black that Wister most directly reflected the period's characteristic acquiescence toward the Jim Crow attitude, an attitude that for Wister would be conducive to returning to the traditional class structure that sustained an aristocracy. In contrast to earlier northerners who wrote of the South, such as De Forest and Tourgée, Wister felt that the Negro could make only limited advances. Augustus makes this clear when he assures Eliza, "It was awful about the negro. It is awful. The young North thinks so just as much as you do. Oh, we shock our old people! We don't expect them to change, but they mustn't expect us not to. And even some of them have begun to whisper a little doubtfully. But never mind them—here's the negro. We can't kick him out. That plan is childish. So, it's like two men having to live in one house. The white man would keep the house in repair, the black would let it rot. Well, the black must take orders from the white. And it will end so." The condition of blacks, he concluded, must be "something between slavery and equality" (*LB*, 205–206).

One of the best examples of Wister's attitudes is in his handling of the so-called Crum incident in *Lady Baltimore*. On December 31, 1902, President Roosevelt had appointed a respected black man, Dr. William D. Crum of Charleston, as port of custom's collector. In spite of the unimportance of this position, the same white Charlestonians who had earlier praised Crum were up in arms, appalled that a black should be placed in a position superior to that of white lady clerks.[31] The fight between Senator "Pitchfork" Ben Tillman of South Carolina and the president over the appointment dragged on until 1904, with Tillman relying on filibustering until Roosevelt went out of office and Taft assured southerners that he would appoint no blacks to office in the South. In the novel Wister is sympathetic to the outrage of white Kings Port over the appointment of this black man. He pictures the young white hero of the novel, John Mayrant, as unfairly demeaned by having to "take orders from a Negro." The narrator, upon learning that Mayrant has engaged in a fight concerning the appointment, comments that Mayrant could not possibly have fought with his black superior—"as well might a nobleman cross swords with a peasant" (*LB*, 123). Wister's strongest indictment of the appointment comes, however, from Daddy Ben, an Uncle Tom creation whom the author

31. For a more complete account of the Crum incident see Francis Butler Simkins, *Pitchfork Ben Tillman, South Carolinian* (Baton Rouge: Louisiana State University Press, 1944), 415–18, and Mason, "Owen Wister: Champion of Old Charleston," 180. The letters Roosevelt wrote to Wister concerning *Lady Baltimore* may be seen in Wister's *Roosevelt* and in E. Morrison (ed.), *The Letters of Theodore Roosevelt*, (7 vols.; Cambridge: Harvard University Press, 1952), V, 221–30.

presents as the "right" kind of Negro—a retainer, loyal to his white families, and indignant at the airs put on by "reconstructed niggers." Daddy Ben reassures John Mayrant, saying, "Mas' John, I speck de Pres*i*dent he dun' know de culled people like we knows 'um, else he nebber bin 'pint dat ar boss in de Cussum House, no, sah" (*LB*, 116).

Roosevelt, in a fifteen-page letter to Wister, praised portions of the novel but in his comments on the Crum incident devastated Wister's "put-upon Southerners" thesis: "These very people whose views you endorse are those who have tried to reintroduce slavery by the infamous system of peonage. . . . I am not satisfied that I acted wisely in either the Booker Washington dinner or the Crum appointment, though each was absolutely justified from every proper standpoint save that of expediency. But the anger against me was just as great in the communities where I acted exactly as the Charlestonians said I ought to act. I know no people in the North so slavishly conventional, so slavishly afraid of expressing any opinion hostile to or different from that held by their neighbors, as is true of the southerners, and most especially of the Charleston aristocrats, on all vital questions. They shriek in public about miscegenation, but they leer as they talk to me privately of the colored mistresses and colored children of white men whom they know." Finally, Roosevelt criticized his friend for his attitudes. "In Lady Baltimore you give what strength you can to those denouncing and opposing the men who are doing their best to bring a little nearer the era of right conduct in the South."[32]

Wister remained unconvinced. In his biography of Roosevelt he commented again on the Crum incident. Appointing Crum, he said, "finished him with those highly spir-

---

32. Wister, *Roosevelt*, 254–56.

ited, sorely bruised people. . . . It was the deep bruise; and the President, meaning well but not aware how sore it was still, had pressed it. It was not the Civil War . . . it was Reconstruction that was the real, lasting bruise."[33]

In addition to the narrator's declaiming and the author's use of actual historical events, the more "fictional" aspects of *Lady Baltimore* also express Wister's favorable attitudes toward the South. The cast of characters—some based on real people, others fictional representatives of "types"—reflect the dichotomy of North and South. It is certainly no accident, I think, that the products of two towns—Newport and Kings Port—are juxtaposed. As the names imply, the visitors from Newport are largely, "new people," the nouveau riche whom Wister deplored as "the lower classes with dollars and no grandfathers, who live in palaces at Newport, and look forward to everything and back to nothing" (*LB*, 5). In contrast, the inhabitants of Kings Port are linked with aristocracy and the past. Indeed, two Kings Port aristocrats are described as analogous to their lovely old city. They are said to be "as narrow as those streets [yet] . . . as lovely as those serene gardens; and if I had smiled at their prejudices, I had loved their innocence, their deep innocence, of the poisoned age which has succeeded their own" (*LB*, 161).

Wister calls Newport inhabitants the "yellow rich," and he directs not one generous remark toward them. They are loud, garish, tacky and, worst of all, are unaware of their vulgarity. They roar into Kings Port in loud, noisy motor cars, disturbing the placidness of the quiet city, and they are bored with the absence of fast life there. Wister describes the approach of these "northern invaders" in much the same way a

---

33. *Ibid.*, 114–15. It should be noted that Wister did make some changes in the novel in accordance with Roosevelt's opinions, but these changes were not extensive.

nineteenth-century southerner might have described Sher-
man's army. Among them are two crass financiers, Charley
and Bohn; Gazza, an "Italian nobleman, who sold old furni-
ture to new Americans"; Kitty, the sister of Charley who is
presently engaged in a divorce so she may marry Bohn; Hortense Rieppe, a southerner who has become northernized
through frequent visits to Newport; and Beverly Rogers, the
only one among the group who is of a good, old family. Only
Beverly, of course, has letters of introduction to any of the
better houses of Kings Port.

The narrator, who has known Beverly before, looks with
horror upon the group, and he explains Beverly's association
with them in pessimistic terms that indict the state of affairs in
the North: "These were the Replacers, whom Beverly's clear-
sighted eyes saw swarming round the temple of his civilization,
pushing down the aisles, climbing over the backs of the
benches, walking over each other's bodies, and seizing those
front seats which his family had sat in since New York had
been New York; and so the wise fellow very prudently took
every step that would insure the Replacers' inviting him to
occupy one of his own chairs" (*LB*, 309). At one point the
narrator compares the Newport crowd to a herd of swine, and
the analogy is reiterated when he says of Kitty that "while she
could feed people, her trough would be well thronged" (*LB*,
308).

The controlling element of the plot, the situation that
has brought this Newport crowd to Kings Port, is a romance—
the engagement of John Mayrant, of ancient Kings Port
ancestry, to Hortense Rieppe, a southerner claiming to be
from Kings Port, said by some to be "from Georgia" (a
terrific indictment in the eyes of Kings Port), and presently
the darling of Newport. Although the courtship is not techni-
cally a North-South one, for all intents and purposes it may be

viewed as such. For Hortense has completely assimilated the manners of Newport, and her stature in Kings Port is decidedly that of an outsider. It is hinted further that although John Mayrant was dazzled by her, as would be any innocent young person on a visit into Newport society, upon returning to the South he has doubts about her but his southern code of ethics prevents him from breaking the engagement.

There is also a triangle aspect to the romance. As the story progresses, we see John increasingly attracted to Eliza La Heu, a young plantation girl of a poor but ancient South Carolina family. Eliza apparently shares John's feelings, but she too considers him bound by his pledge to Hortense, and, accordingly, the relationship seems permanently thwarted.

Thus the author shows clearly the conflicting forces. John Mayrant is the epitome of a southern gentleman—handsome, noble, ready to fight to defend his honor, and willing to die before compromising it. He is genteelly impoverished, but has inherited a phosphate claim which may make him rich (and which Hortense has brought down her financier friends to assess). Hortense, despite her association with the "yellow rich," is indeed alluring—the narrator dwells at length upon the perfection of her dress and hair, the splendid modulation of her voice—qualities that make her appear more stunning than Eliza La Heu. It seems too that although she prefers John as a wealthy husband and is guilty of playing him off against other suitors, she is deeply in love with him. But Wister colors this love with an unusual quality when he has Hortense reveal to Kitty that she loves John most for his "innocence." Hortense is worldly, and what appeals to her in John is the very quality she herself lacks.

The narrator, of course, favors Eliza over Hortense. Of Hortense he says, "She had at length betrayed something which her skill and the intricate enamel of her experience had hitherto, and with entire success, concealed—namely, the latent vulgarity of the woman" (LB, 283). Thus, the two women are dramatically different: "[Hortense] was wearing, for the sake of Kings Port, her best behavior, her most knowing form, and, indeed, it was a well-done imitation of the real thing; it would last through most occasions, and it would deceive most people. But here was the trouble: she was *wearing* it; while, through the whole encounter, Eliza La Heu had worn nothing but her natural and perfect dignity" (LB, 283).

The affair appears at an impasse, and the day of the wedding is approaching rapidly when Hortense unwittingly releases John from his bond. While they are spending a morning on Charley's yacht in Kings Port harbor, Hortense perversely jumps overboard to show herself a sport. John saves her and, in restoring her life to her, is released from further obligation.

Lady Baltimore draws to an end with two weddings. Hortense marries the wealthy Charley, and, to the narrator's delight, after a respectable waiting period Eliza and John are married. In describing the two weddings Wister puts the finishing touches on his theme, noting that if you did not happen to see the newspaper account of the first wedding, "just read the account of the next wedding that occurs among the New York yellow rich, and you will know how Charley and Hortense were married." In contrast, "The marriage of Eliza La Heu and John Mayrant was of a different quality; no paper pronounced it 'up to date'. . . . This marriage was *solemnized*" (LB, 385, 387).

On this note Wister concludes, and the implication is that things have ended as they should. Kings Port has through this marriage withstood, for a while at least, contamination from the yellow rich, Newport, and the North in general, where "the soul of Uncle Sam has turned into a dollar inside his great, big, strong, triumphant flesh" (LB, 327).

But if Kings Port still endures through personalities like John and Eliza, its endurance is tenuous. Wister argues in the novel that in some ways it is the very poverty, the devastation of the post-Civil War South that has saved it from the rampant commercialism and tawdriness of the Gilded Age. For it is money—industrial money, finance, middle-class money—that destroys the fabric of gracious living. And Kings Port's very tenuousness leads Wister into the idealization we have seen in such writers as Woolson and Hearn: "Dreams, a land of dreams, where even the high noon itself was dreamy; a melting together of earth and air and water in one eternal gentleness of revery!" (*LB*, 249).

One can imagine the author walking through the quiet narrow streets of Charleston with his friend Henry James, each sympathetic to those qualities that set this city apart from bustling New York, flamboyant Newport. Wister, like Woolson and Hearn, could unreservedly praise what he saw without fear of offense to his northern readers. And this praise came easily for him in *Lady Baltimore*, for in this novel, unlike in *The Virginian*, he could picture a dream, an ideal, an alternative to the North, without sacrificing the tradition, the sense of the past which was so important to him. With Kings Port and its inhabitants, Wister again evoked an ideal—an affirmation of a time and place where life is at its finest.

Coda

∽

Henry James in
Charleston

Owen Wister delighted in his role as guide and host to his illustrious friend, Henry James, during James's 1905 visit to Charleston. As we saw in the preceding chapter, Wister was able to provide an "insider's" point of view of the weathered but lovely old city. The fact that James's account of his impressions there is similar in many ways to Wister's picture of Charleston reflects, no doubt, the influence of his guide.

Yet it would be unfair to assume that James merely adopted Wister's prosouthern attitudes. His essay on Charleston in *The American Scene* (1907) may be compared to his earlier writing about the South, which was also sympathetic to southern ways. If James, like Wister, idealized the aristocratic qualities of the South as contrasted with the increasing commercialization of the Northeast, it is because both men shared a vision of the South as a last holdout against vulgarity.

In his idealized treatment of the region, James may be linked with those other nonsoutherners—Stowe, De Forest, Tourgée, Woolson, Hearn, and, of course Wister—who came to the South and wrote about it. But of this group, James is the writer with the most established reputation, the only one, indeed, to have achieved critical recognition as a major talent. It seems appropriate, then, to conclude with his observations to suggest how the matter struck a major literary figure. Not surprisingly, much of his writing about the South reflects a polish and sense of distillation often lacking in the work of the other writers.

The most direct statement of James's vision of the South is his account in *The American Scene* of his journey in the Northeast and the South during 1904 and 1905. Wright Morris notes that James is consciously self-conscious, recording the impressions not of a traveler, but of a native who has finally become aware of what he feels.[1] In his assessment of early twentieth-century America, however, James did reflect to some degree an outsider's point of view, since he had been away for twenty years. The aristocratic values he had taken with him and nurtured in Europe colored his evaluation. Leon Edel, in his introduction to *The American Scene,* points out the changes James "discovered" upon his return. The American continent, still being explored when he had gone abroad, was now being plundered, and with the rapid growth of commerce and industry came the rise of the tycoon and robber baron. James returned to find a new aristocracy founded on wealth, still raw with greed and exploitation.[2]

Although James's portrayal of the South is characterized by restraint, a comparison of his view of it with what he wrote of the North reveals his belief that only the South retained vestiges of a resistance to the general crassness of the age.[3] In his pictures of New York and Newport he presents a vision of the Gilded Age. New York has not only succumbed to, but is the embodiment of, commercialism and materialism. The homes

1. Wright Morris, "Henry James's *The American Scene,*" *Texas Quarterly,* I (Summer-Autumn, 1958), 28.
2. Henry James, *The American Scene,* intro. by Leon Edel (Bloomington: Indiana University Press, 1968), xi. Hereinafter, references to this work will be cited parenthetically in the text.
3. Although Edel implies in his introduction that there were few elements in American society that offset James's disappointment in the American scene, to this reader, James's evaluation of the South seems an exception.

there reflect "the crudity of wealth," and James speaks of "the houses and their candid look of having cost as much as they knew how" (AS, 11). The skyscrapers in New York City are "impudently new and still more impudently 'novel'—this in common with so many other terrible things in America" (AS, 76). In a description of New York that could serve as his definitive statement on the Gilded Age, James lamented the encroachment of materialism: "The very sign of its energy is that it doesn't believe in itself; it fails to succeed, even at a cost of millions, in persuading you that it does. Its mission would appear to be, exactly, to gild the temporary, with its gold, as many inches thick as may be, and then, with a fresh shrug, a shrug of its splendid cynicism for its freshly detected inability to convince, give up its actual work, however exorbitant, as the merest of stop-gaps" (AS, 110).

But it is in James's account of Newport (also the focus of Wister's criticism in *Lady Baltimore*), once a stronghold of the upper class, now, like New York, a victim of the encroaching nouveau riche, that his strongest statement concerning the lost ideals of a finer way of life appears. James compares the old Newport to "a little bare, white, open hand, with slightly-parted fingers, for the observer with a presumed sense for hands to take or to leave. The observer with a real sense never failed to pay this image the tribute of quite tenderly grasping the hand, and even of raising it, delicately, to his lips; having no less, at the same time, the instinct of not shaking it too hard, and that above all of never putting it to any rough work" (AS, 210). In contrast, the mob of new people have failed to perceive the inherent charm of Newport—the "opportunity for escaping the summer heat of other places." Instead, "the pink palm being empty . . . to their vision, they had begun, from far back, to put things into it, things of their own, and of all sorts, and of many ugly, and of more and more expensive, sorts." Lacking vision, the encroachers have heaped up mansions "oddly out of proportion to the scale of nature and of space" (AS, 211).

The old Newport was not like this: "It was the time of settled possession, and yet furthest removed from these blank days in which margin has been consumed and the palaces, on the sites but the other day beyond price, stare silently seaward, monuments to the *blasé* state of their absent proprietors" (AS, 221–22). In a passage curiously like a description of Charleston in Wister's *Lady Baltimore*, James compared the streets of Newport to the walks of old ladies: "The small silver whistle of the past, with its charming quaver of weak gaiety, quite played the tune I asked of it up and down the tiny, sunny, empty Newport vistas, perspectives coming to a stop like the very short walks of very old ladies. What indeed but little very old ladies did they resemble, the little very old streets?" (AS, 215). This vision of an earlier Newport is, however, now only a mirage; the actualization of it could be found (as it had been by Wister) only in Charleston.

James's descriptions of New York and Newport show the evils of the mistaken belief held by the nouveau riche that gold can buy beauty and charm. As James noted, "Charm is a flower of wild and windblown seed—often not to be counted on when most anxiously planted, but taking its own time and its own place both for enriching and for mocking us. It mocks assuredly, above all, our money and our impatience, elements addressed to buying or 'ordering' it, and only asks that when it does come we shall know it and love it" (AS, 239). Owen Wister implied in *Lady Baltimore* that it was the poverty of the South that enabled it to retain its charm. And James, in his evaluation, would seem to agree. Waiting at a junction for the train that would take him to Charleston, he began to succumb to the South's magic:

I had succeeded in artlessly becoming a perfectly isolated traveller, with nobody to warn or comfort me, with nobody even to command. But it was precisely in this situation that I felt again, as by the click of a spring, that my adventure had, in spite of everything, or perhaps indeed just because of everything, a charm all its own—and a charm, moreover, which I was to have from that moment, for any connection, no difficulty whatever in recognizing. It must have broken out more particularly, then and there, in the breath of the night, which was verily now the bland air of the South—mild, benignant, a benediction in itself as it hung about me, and with that blest quality in it of its appearing a medium through which almost any good might come. It was the air of the open gates—not, like that of the North, of the closed; and one inhaled it, in short, on the spot, as the very boon of one's quest.

A couple of hours later, in the right train, which had at last arrived, I had so settled to submission to this spell that it had wrought for me, I think, all its magic—ministered absolutely to the maximum of suggestion, which became thus, for my introduction to Charleston, the presiding influence (*AS*, 400–401).

His first impression of Charleston was that it would be something different from his northern experiences: "Charleston early in the morning, on my driving from the station, was, it had to be admitted, no very finished picture, but at least, already, it was different—ever so different in aspect and 'feeling,' and above all for intimation and suggestion, from any passage of the American scene as yet deciphered" (*AS*, 402). Although upon entering the South James had noted its contrast to the North—"It is astonishing, along the Atlantic coast, how, from the moment the North ceases to insist, the South may begin to presume" (*AS*, 303)—and cited the essence of the old southern idea in Richmond, it is in Charleston that he formed his clearest picture of the Old South. He had been unable to view Richmond without allowing his response to be colored by the ideology of the Civil War; he felt compelled to point out the racial prejudices of a young Virginian he encountered, and he pronounced the onetime capital of the Confederacy a pathetic thing. Charleston was another matter. The sight of an elderly mulatto "just barely held open for me a door through which I felt I might have looked straight and far back into the past. The past, that of the vanished order, was hanging on there behind her—as much of it as the scant place would accommodate" (AS, 403). He admitted, "I was to find myself liking, in the South and in the most monstrous fashion, it appeared, those aspects in which the consequences of the great folly were, for extent and gravity, still traceable. . . . And this, I need hardly say, from a point of view having so little in common with the vindictive as to be quite directly opposed to it." These things, he said, had been through the fire. "They at least are not cheerful rawnesses—they have been baked beautiful and hard" (AS, 404-405).

James qualified his praise, citing the scantiness, the poverty of Charleston. Upon leaving the city, he was not too enchanted to refrain from grumbling over "the inimitable detachment with which . . . the negro porter . . . put straight down into the mud of the road the dressing-bag I was obliged, a few minutes later, in our close-pressed company, to nurse on my knees" (AS, 423). He acknowledged that the southern cause had been hopeless and that there was an oppressive thinness to the southern scene, yet there remains in this work an insistence that of all the segments of American society, only in the South was the ideal even approached. In his concluding statement on Charleston, a description of St. Michael's Church, James asserts:

The high, complicated, inflated spire of the church has the sincerity, approved of time, that is so rare, over the land, in the work of man's hands, laden though these be with the millions he offers as a vain bribe to it; and in the sweet old churchyard ancient authority seemed to me, on the occasion of my visit, to sit, among the sun-

warmed tombs and the interrelated slabs and the extravagant flowers, as on the sole cushion the general American bareness in such
connections had left it. There was more still of association and
impression; I found, under this charm, I confess, character in every
feature. Even in the much-maintained interior revolutions and re-
novations have respected its sturdy, rather sombre essence: the place
feels itself, in the fine old dusky archaic way, the constituted temple
of a faith—achieves, in a word, the air of reality that one had seen
in every other such case, from town to town and from village to
village, missed with an unconsciousness that had to do duty for
success (*AS*, 421).

One need only compare this with James's statements about the
North, and the contrast becomes clear.

In an article, "Henry James's Fable of Carolina," Charles R.
Anderson comments on James's treatment of South Carolina
in *The Reverberator* and the novelette, *Pandora*. Noting that
these works illustrate the author's idealism of the South, he
makes the interesting observation that James's view was not
corrected by his actual observation of the South twenty years
later. On the contrary, the earlier vision *colored* the impressions he recorded in *The American Scene*. [4] A similar statement
might also be made concerning *The Bostonians* (1886), which
also presents an idealized version of the South through the
characterization of the protagonist, Basil Ransom. But an
ideal can (and perhaps must) exist in the face of reality. Thus
the fact that James had a preconceived notion of the South
that was not shattered by his later visit there gives support to
the thesis of the necessity of an idealized counterpoint to the
humdrum North.

Before looking at *The Bostonians* we might note that James's
friend Howells, who visited the South a number of times in

4. Charles R. Anderson, "Henry James's Fable of Carolina," *South Atlantic Quarterly*, LIV (1955), 249.

the eighties and nineties, also pictured it favorably in *A Hazard of New Fortunes*. Not only had Howells' ire against England for its support of the South during the war abated by this time, his attitudes toward the South itself had so softened that he was able to treat its representatives in the novel, Colonel Woodburne and his daughter, in a comic yet sympathetic way. These two are presented as types—the old chivalric South and the new (modeled after the commercial North)—and thus they never come to life as real people. But in spite of the comic overtones, Howells idealizes the colonel, allowing him to play the role of peacemaker and even causing the practical, profit-seeking Fulkerson to echo the colonel's belief "there ain't anything left of that Walter Scott dignity and chivalry in the rising generation."[5]

Howells touches upon this might-have-been aspect of the South most closely when he describes Miss Woodburne's feelings about her silver-headed father: "The broken Southern past, sentimentally dear to him, and practically absurd to her. No such South as he remembered had ever existed to her knowledge, and no such civilisation as he imagined would ever exist, to her belief, anywhere."[6] Even if the colonel is only a stock character, in Howells' depiction of his sense of honor, integrity, and chivalry, he appears superior to representatives of both the New South and its model, the North.

The southerner, Basil Ransom, in *The Bostonians*, is also caricatured. However, James goes far beyond Howells in his condemnation of the North and the resulting idealization of the South. *The Bostonians*, despite its northern setting, is relevant to our purposes in terms of the comparisons made in the novel through James's use of the North-South romance motif.

5. William D. Howells, *A Hazard of New Fortunes* (2 vols.; New York: Harper and Brothers, 1889), II, 53.
6. *Ibid.*, II, 177.

The major action centers around the struggle between Olive Chancellor, Boston spinster and supporter of the women's movement, and her cousin, Basil Ransom, southern conservative, for control and possession of a strikingly beautiful young girl, Verena Tarrant. Whether the contest is considered a sexual one, the battle of liberalism versus conservative philosophy, or of the feminine versus the masculine principle, the importance of the struggle lies in the fact that the victor is the southerner.[7]

Although it has been argued that James's ambivalence about the South is reflected in his erratic treatment of Basil, who appears sometimes as knight in shining armor, at other times as a pompous fool, the fact remains that he does win Verena. When his portrayal is compared to James's picture of Olive Chancellor, there can be no doubt that the treatment of Basil is more flattering than that of his Boston cousin.[8] Olive is a spinster, "unmarried by every implication of her being. She was a spinster as Shelley was a lyric poet, or as the month of August is sultry. . . . She had absolutely no figure, and presented a certain appearance of feeling cold. With all this, there was something very modern and highly developed in her aspect; she had the advantages as well as the drawbacks of a nervous organization."[9] At dinner with her, Basil discovers that although Olive smiled, she never laughed. "Later, he saw that she was a woman without laughter; exhilaration, if it ever

7. See discussions of The Bostonians by the following: Lionel Trilling, The Opposing Self: Nine Essays in Criticism (New York: Viking Press, 1955); Louise Bogan, "The Portrait of New England," Nation, CXLVI (April 23, 1938), 471–74; Pelham Edgar, Henry James: Man and Author (London: Grant Richards, 1925).

8. In "James's Portrait of the Southerner," American Literature, XXVII (1955), 309–31, Charles R. Anderson discusses at length ambiguities in the characterization of Basil Ransom.

9. Henry James, The Bostonians (New York: Dial Press, 1945), 14–15. Hereinafter, references to this work will be cited parenthetically in the text.

visited her, was dumb" (B, 15). Life for Olive consists not of pleasure, but duty. Basil dichotomizes "the people who take things hard and the people who take them easy. He perceived very quickly that Miss Chancellor belonged to the former class" (B, 7–8).

Olive is neurotic, unpleasant, and generally unappealing, and James presents an appropriate setting for her in a Boston that is in a period of decline after its heroic age. Once the hub of humanitarian zeal, the city is now at ebbtide, in the throes of stagnation. Van Wyck Brooks notes that for James, who had no hereditary associations with Boston and who saw its smallness in comparison with the great world, the city seemed "now in its hour of Gotterdammerung, Boston was nothing if not repellent."[10]

The supporting characters reinforce this view. Olive's friend, Miss Birdseye (modeled after Elizabeth Palmer Peabody), at first appears to be an unselfish humanitarian. But James soon tells the reader that she is "a confused, entangled, inconsequent, discursive old woman, whose charity began at home and ended nowhere" (B, 22). Commenting on the fact that since the Civil War she has been deprived of her occupation as abolitionist, he muses, "It would have been a nice question whether, in her heart of hearts, for the sake of this excitement, she did not sometimes wish the blacks back in bondage" (B, 23). The portraits of other Bostonians, supporters of the women's movement, are also unflattering. Dr. Tarrant is a man of dubious talents. Burrage, Verena's suitor, seems a milksop, still under the control of his mother. The newspaper man, Matthias Pardon, loves publicity above all. Each of these characters seems sterile and artificial.

10. Van Wyck Brooks, "Henry James: The American Scene," *Dial,* LXXV (July, 1923), 34.

In contrast to this stands the masculine Basil Ransom, and James's choice of the virile young southerner as protagonist is significant. He had originally decided on a western hero but rejected this plan for several reasons. For one thing, feminism had made far more progress in the West where new social ideas were more easily established. Thus the West could hardly be established as a counterpoint to Boston. In addition, the qualities associated with a western hero, such as being free from tradition, unencumbered with intellectual refinement, and blessed with material success, would not have served James's purposes. As Lionel Trilling notes, by involving the feminist movement with the struggle between North and South, he made clear that his story was dealing with a cultural crisis.[11]

Ransom serves not only as Olive Chancellor's opponent but as a contrast to the values of Boston society in general. He comes from an aristocratic society unlike that of New England; in fact he is in some ways, like James, an American European. An avid reader of De Tocqueville and Carlyle, he deplores the "confusion of judgment" he finds rampant in the democratic North.[12] In addition to his qualities as southern aristocrat and conservative, Basil exudes a vitality that is lacking in the Bostonians. For although he believes in the natural energy of northerners, Ransom later discovers that "few Northerners were, in their secret soul, so energetic as he" (B, 13). This vitality for life is contrasted throughout the novel with Olive's coldness. Even the settings of Olive's and Basil's courtship of Verena illustrate this contrast of frigidity and passion. Unlike Olive, who tutors Verena on cold, snowy nights in her cloistered parlor, Basil woos her in the brilliant

11. Lionel Trilling, "The Bostonians," in *The Opposing Self*, 111–12.

12. Robert Emmet Long, "The Society and the Masks: *The Blithdale Romance* and *The Bostonians*," *Nineteenth Century Fiction*, XIX (September, 1964), 113.

daylight of Central Park. Olive is numb to the appeal of nature, as the scene in the park indicates, but it is here that Basil makes the strongest case of his love. Thus, in his use of park and seashore settings James makes evident the Arcadian nature of the love affair.[13] Even though Basil has been transplanted from South to North in order to make his fortune, he is associated with the appeal of warmth and the out-of-doors—qualities typically associated with the South.

James presents Verena Tarrant, the object of contention between Basil and Olive, as an empty vessel, an instrument used by her parents and others for their own purposes. Verena has a gift for impromptu speaking and, after being "started up" by her father, is able to talk at length on such subjects as the sufferings and the rights of women. Basil and Olive see her for the first time in Miss Birdseye's parlor, and here the contest between them begins. Olive's idea is to train and polish Verena so that she may use her gift of speaking as an instrument for the women's movement. She tells Verena, "You must move the world with it; it's divine" (B, 70).

Ransom's interest in Verena is very different. He views Verena's speech as charming but "pretty moonshine ... monstrous sentiments." James remarks that "Basil Ransom made his reflections on the crazy character of the age in which such a performance as that was treated as an intellectual effort, a contribution to a question." Verena "counted as a factor only because the public mind was in a muddle ... she was meant for something divinely different—for privacy, for him, for love" (B, 227). Basil's wish to enjoy Verena in private is similar to his attitudes about his native South. He declines to talk about his home, wishing "to leave her alone

13. Robert C. McLean, "*The Bostonians:* New England Pastoral," *Papers on Language and Literature,* VII (1971), 376.

with her wounds and her memories, not prating in the market-place either of her troubles or her hopes" (B, 42). Similarly, Verena is to be kept privately, not dangled before the public.

Olive "buys" Verena for a year by settling her parents with a large sum of money. But during this period, Basil, in his interviews with Verena at Cambridge, Central Park, and Cape Cod, is able to "win" her through his passion. The result is a conversion on Verena's part from her position as spokesman for the women's movement, to love for Basil. "The words he had spoken to her . . . about her genuine vocation, as distinguished from the hollow and factitious ideal with which her family and her association with Olive Chancellor had saddled her—these words, the most effective and penetrating he had uttered, had sunk into her soul and worked and fermented there. She had come at last to believe them, and that was the alteration, the transformation" (B, 323). Basil's victory required much of Verena: "She was to burn everything she had adored; she was to adore everything she had burned." For Verena, "It was simply that the truth had changed sides." James states that "it was always passion, in fact; but now the object was other" (B, 323–24).

Verena's renunciation of Olive and the women's movement takes place in the final scene in the music hall where Verena is to make the speech that will launch her as the spokesman of the movement. In this scene which has been referred to as a refought battle of North and South, Basil sweeps Verena away as Olive runs out to sacrifice herself to the angry audience. His triumph is now complete.

Like Owen Wister, Henry James despaired over the loss of a finer age, of an aristocracy with a developed sense of taste. Both felt that, whether North or South, the aristocracy shared a bond that separated it from the common man, the vulgar herd. Olive and Basil, people of good breeding, regret the tawdriness of the present time. Although their values are different, they share a sense of loss at the passing of a more noble, heroic past.[14] If this is so, then it becomes even more significant that Ransom is the victor in the novel. For James seems to be saying, then, as did Wister, that it is only in the southern ideal, represented here by Basil, that a sense of "the better life, the high ideals" may be retained. The Northeast has sold itself in the marketplace (much as Olive, at the conclusion of the novel, prostrates herself to the angry mob), and the only hope lies in Ransom's offer of privacy to Verena.

In the concluding lines of *The Bostonians* Verena tells Basil that she is glad he has taken her away: "But though she was glad, he presently discovered that, beneath her hood, she was in tears. It is to be feared that with the union, so far from brilliant, into which she was about to enter, these were not the last she was destined to shed" (B, 378). James again reveals the tenuousness of the ideal he has postulated, and the ambiguity of Verena's situation reflects his own awareness that the South has only a shaky hold on that which has been completely lost in the North. Yet in the twenty-odd years between the inception of *The Bostonians* and the completion of *The American Scene*, James retained a vision of the South as a place apart from the increasingly corrupt Northeast. The "thinness" of Charleston notwithstanding, it held fast to the gentility and fineness which in the rest of the nation were sorely missed.

Writing about Lafcadio Hearn, Elizabeth Stevenson remarks that it was just when "responsible Southern leaders were try-

14. David Howard, "The Bostonians," in John Goode (ed.), *The Air of Reality: New Essays on Henry James* (London: Methuen, 1972), 67. Howard refers to Olive and Basil as "the two chief discriminators of the age."

ing to make the South a little more like the North, that the
lagging, behind-the-times South became an appropriate place
for the imagination of the North."[15] And James commented
upon the "strange feminization" of the postwar South. These
conflicting desires to northernize and subordinate yet to preserve the past also characterize the changes that took place in
northern writing about the South from the time De Forest
wrote *Miss Ravenel's Conversion* until the publication of Wister's *Lady Baltimore.*

De Forest's Lillie Ravenel, evolving from plucky rebel to
pliant, submissive helpmeet to Colburne and convert to the
North, personified the desired subordination of the South to
northern ways. Although Tourgée converted male southerners—the sex he felt could best take an active role in Reconstruction—in his novels, he also reflected the mood of
reform and submission of the time. But, as Stevenson notes,
even if Reconstruction ultimately failed, the South had
learned one lesson from the ideas of such northerners as De
Forest and Tourgée—life could not return to the prewar state.
The usurping of the old system of slavery brought with it a
change in the economy. The South would turn to industry for
money; cities and towns would grow as labor congregated to
industrial centers. Former plantation owners and other ambitious men would become the heads of a new paternal
system—the factory.

Thus, Woolson's Garda Thorne became a compelling symbol of what was rapidly being lost throughout the nation, even
in the South—the uniqueness of an old, aristocratic way of
life. Accordingly, Hearn's affirmation of the beauty and sensuality of the South, symbolized by Chita's transformation

---

15. Elizabeth Stevenson, *Lafcadio Hearn* (New York: Macmillan, 1961), 141–
142.

from child of society to child of nature, and Wister's warnings of the importance of avoiding northern corruption, culminating in the marriage of southerners Eliza La Heu and John Mayrant, illustrate the diverse yet complementary forms this idealization of the South in fiction could assume. That even the cautious James succumbed as much as he did to the charms of old Charleston lends credence to this portrayal of the South as a "might-be" land.

From the very first there are suggestions that the South embodied for each of these writers the possibility of life on a higher plane. Reading their works, one can view the growth of this concept from implicit, unconscious suggestion in *Uncle Tom's Cabin* to the dominant motif of such works as *Chita* or *Lady Baltimore.* The process was not unique with these writers, but they all share certain characteristics—each coming to the South from the North and writing during the years in which concern with the South reached the highest levels in history. For the most part they are transitional writers, continuing some of the traditions of the earlier plantation fiction, setting groundwork for the southern renaissance when concern with the South would evolve into a more sophisticated treatment of the workings of individual consciousness. But they are important as a unit; for in their work is reflected the changing attitudes of the nation toward the South, and this change from criticism to acceptance and fascination marked the emergence of something that had existed from the beginning—the cultivation of a longing for splendor, a dream that in the enchanted country life *was* somehow different.

Selected
Bibliography

PRIMARY WORKS

De Forest, John William. *The Bloody Chasm.* New York: D. Appleton, 1881.

_____. "Charleston Under Arms." *Atlantic Monthly,* VII (April, 1861), 488–505.

_____. "The Colored Member." *Galaxy,* XIII (March, 1872), 293–302.

_____. "The Duchesne Estate." *Galaxy,* VII (June, 1869), 823–35.

_____. *European Acquaintance: Being Sketches of People in Europe.* New York: Harper and Brothers, 1858.

_____. "Fate Ferguston." *Galaxy,* III (January, 1867), 87–100.

_____. "A Gentleman of the Old School." *Atlantic Monthly,* XXI (May, 1868), 546–55.

_____. "The Great American Novel." *Nation,* VI (January 9, 1868), 27–29.

_____. "The 'High-Toned Gentleman.'" *Nation,* VI (March 12, 1868), 206–208.

_____. *The History of the Indians of Connecticut from the Earliest Known Period to 1850.* Hartford: W. J. Hammersley [sic], 1851.

_____ "An Independent Ku Klux." *Galaxy,* XIII (April, 1872), 480–88.

_____. *Kate Beaumont.* 1872. Reprint. State College, Pa.: Bald Eagle Press, 1963.

_____. "Lieutenant Barker's Ghost Story." *Harper's,* XXXIX (October, 1869), 713–20.

_____. *Miss Ravenel's Conversion from Secession to Loyalty.* Columbus, Ohio: Charles E. Merrill, 1969.

_____. "A Night at Sea." *Harper's,* XXXIX (July, 1869), 195–202.

————. *Oriental Acquaintance: or, Letters from Syria.* New York: Dix, Edwards, 1856.

————. "Parole d'Honneur." *Harper's,* XXXVII (August–September, 1868), 372–78, 483–90.

————. *Poems: Medley and Palestrina.* New Haven: Tuttle, Morehouse, and Taylor, 1902.

————. "Rum Creeters is Women." *Harper's,* XXXIV (March, 1867), 484–91.

————. *Seacliff.* Boston: Phillips, Sampson, 1859.

————. *A Union Officer in the Reconstruction.* Edited by James H. Croushore and David M. Potter. New Haven: Yale University Press, 1948.

————. *A Volunteer's Adventures: A Union Captain's Record of the Civil War.* Edited by James H. Croushore. New Haven: Yale University Press, 1946.

————. "Was It a Ghost?" New York *Times,* (January 17, 1875), 3.

————. "Witching Times. A Novel in Thirty Chapters." *Putnam's Monthly Magazine,* VIII–X (December, 1856–September, 1857).

Hearn, Lafcadio. *An American Miscellany: Articles and Stories Now First Collected.* Edited by Albert Mordell. 2 vols. New York: Dodd, Mead, 1924.

————. *Chita: A Memory of Last Island.* 1889. Reprint. Chapel Hill: University of North Carolina Press, 1969.

————. *Creole Sketches.* Edited by Charles Woodward Hutson. Boston: Houghton Mifflin, 1924.

————. *Editorials.* Edited by Charles Woodward Hutson. Boston: Houghton Mifflin, 1926.

————. *Essays in European and Oriental Literature.* Edited by Albert Mordell. New York: Dodd, Mead, 1923.

————. *Essays on American Literature.* Edited by Sanki Ichikawa. Tokyo: Hokuseido Press, 1929.

————. *Facts and Fancies.* Edited by R. Tanabé. Tokyo: Hokuseido Press, 1929.

————. *Fantastics and Other Fancies.* Edited by Charles Woodward Hutson. Boston: Houghton Mifflin, 1914.

————. *Gombo Zhèbes* or *Little Dictionary of Creole Proverbs.* New York: Will H. Coleman, 1885.

————. *Historical Sketch Book and Guide to New Orleans and Environs.* New York: Will H. Coleman, 1885.

————. *Interpretations of Literature.* Edited by John Erskine. 2 vols. New York: Dodd, Mead, 1915.

————. *La Cuisine Creole: A Collection of Culinary Recipes from Leading Chefs and Noted Creole Housewives, Who Have Made New Orleans Famous for Its Cuisine.* New York: Will H. Coleman, 1885.

————. *Letters from the Raven: Being the Correspondence of Lafcadio Hearn with Henry Watkin.* Edited by Milton Bronner. New York: Albert and Charles Boni, 1930.

————. *Life and Literature.* Edited by John Erskine. New York: Dodd, Mead, 1917.

————. *Occidental Gleanings.* Edited by Albert Mordell. 2 vols. New York: Dodd, Mead, 1925.

————. "An Orange Christmas." New Orleans: Paul Veith, 1914.

————. *Some Chinese Ghosts.* Boston: Roberts Brothers, 1887.

————. "Some Martinique Letters of Lafcadio Hearn." Edited by Elizabeth Bisland. *Harper's,* CXLII (March, 1921), 516–25.

————. *Stray Leaves from Strange Literature.* Boston: James R. Osgood, 1884.

————. *Talks to Writers.* Edited by John Erskine. New York: Dodd, Mead, 1920.

————. *Two Years in the French West Indies.* New York: Harper and Brothers, 1890.

————. *The Writings of Lafcadio Hearn.* 16 vols. Boston: Houghton Mifflin, 1923.

————. *Youma: The Story of a West-Indian Slave.* New York: Harper and Brothers, 1890.

James, Henry. *The American Scene.* Bloomington: Indiana University Press, 1968.

————. *The Bostonians.* New York: Dial Press, 1945.

————. *Partial Portraits.* London: Macmillan, 1888.

King, Edward. *The Great South.* Edited by W. Magruder Drake and Robert R. Jones. Baton Rouge: Louisiana State University Press, 1972.

Stowe, Harriet Beecher. *Dred: A Tale of the Great Dismal Swamp.* 2 vols. Boston: Phillips, Sampson, 1856.

————. *Palmetto Leaves.* Boston: James R. Osgood, 1873.

————. *Uncle Tom's Cabin.* 1852. Reprint. Garden City, N.Y.: Doubleday, 1960.

Tourgée, Albion W. *An Appeal to Caesar.* New York: Fords, Howard, and Hulbert, 1884.

———. *Bricks Without Straw.* Edited by Otto H. Olsen. Baton Rouge: Louisiana State University Press, 1969.

———. ["The 'C' Letters."] *North State,* March-July, 1878 [published anonymously].

———. Notes and decision to *The Code of Civil Procedure of North Carolina.* Raleigh: John Nichols, 1878.

———. "The Education of the Negro." *Congregationalist,* XXXIII (November 30, 1881), 389.

———. "The Effect of the Northern Elections at the South." *National Anti-Slavery Standard,* XXVIII (November 9, 1867), [1] [signed "Wenckar"].

———. *A Fool's Errand.* New York: Fords, Howard, and Hulbert, 1879.

———. *Hot Plowshares.* New York: Fords, Howard, and Hulbert, 1883.

———. *The Invisible Empire.* 1880. Reprint. Ridgewood, N.J.: Gregg Press, 1968.

———. *John Eax and Mamelon; or, the South Without the Shadow.* New York: Fords, Howard, and Hulbert, 1882.

———. "The Right to Vote." *Forum,* VIII (March, 1890), 78–92.

———. *A Royal Gentleman.* Published as *Toinette,* 1874. Reprint. Ridgewood, N. J.: Gregg Press, 1967.

———. "Shall White Minorities Rule?" *Forum,* VII (April, 1889), 143–55.

———. "The South as a Field for Fiction." *Forum,* VI (December, 1888), 404–13.

———. *The Story of a Thousand. Being a History of the Service of the 105th Ohio Volunteer Infantry, in the War for the Union from August 21, 1862, to June 6, 1865.* Buffalo: S. McGerald and Son, 1896.

———. *Union Register* (Greensboro, N.C.), January 3–June 14, 1867.

———. "What Will Be the Result?" *National Anti-Slavery Standard,* XXVIII (October 19, 1867), [1], [Signed "Wenckar"].

Wister, Owen. "Hank's Woman." *Harper's Weekly,* XXXVI (August 27, 1892), 821–23.

———. "How Lin McLean Went East." *Harper's Magazine,* LXXXVI (December, 1892), 135–46.

_____. *Lady Baltimore*. 1905. Reprint. Ridgewood, N.J.: Gregg Press, 1968.

_____. *Roosevelt: The Story of a Friendship, 1880–1919*. New York: Macmillan, 1930.

_____. *The Virginian*. New York: Macmillan, 1902.

Woolson, Constance Fenimore. "The Ancient City." *Harper's*, L (December, 1874, January, 1875), 1–25, 165–85.

_____. *Anne*. New York: Harper and Brothers, 1882.

_____. "Barnaby Pass." *Harper's*, LV (July, 1877), 261–71.

_____. "Black Point." *Harper's*, LIX (June, 1879), 84–97.

_____. "'Bro.'" *Appleton's Journal*, n.s., V (November, 1878), 417–28.

_____. *Castle Nowhere: Lake-Country Sketches*. Boston: J. R. Osgood, 1875.

_____. "Crowder's Cove: A Story of the War." *Appleton's Journal*, XV (March 18, 1876), 357–62.

_____. *Dorothy and other Italian Stories*. New York: Harper and Brothers, 1896.

_____. *East Angels*. New York: Harper and Brothers, 1886.

_____. "Felipa." *Lippincott's Magazine*, XVII (June, 1876), 702–13.

_____. "The Florida Beach." *Galaxy*, XVIII (October, 1874), 482–83.

_____. *For the Major*. New York: Harper and Brothers, 1883.

_____. *For the Major and Selected Short Stories*. Edited by Rayburn S. Moore. New Haven: College and University Press, 1967.

_____. "The French Broad." *Harper's*, L (April, 1875), 617–36.

_____. *The Front Yard and Other Italian Stories*. New York: Harper and Brothers, 1895.

_____. *Horace Chase*. New York: Harper and Brothers, 1894.

_____. "In Search of the Picturesque." *Harper's*, XLV (July, 1872), 161–68.

_____. "In the Cotton Country." *Appleton's Journal*, XV (April 29, 1876), 547–51.

_____. *Jupiter Lights*. New York: Harper and Brothers, 1889.

_____. "King David." *Scribner's*, XV (April, 1878), 781–89.

_____. *Mentone, Cairo, and Corfu*. New York: Harper and Brothers, 1896.

_____. "Miss Vedder." *Harper's*, LVIII (March, 1879), 590–601.

_____. "The Oklawaha." *Harper's*, LII (January, 1876), 161–79.

———. "Old Gardiston." *Harper's,* LII (April, 1876), 662–74.

———. "Rodman the Keeper." *Atlantic Monthly,* XXXIX (March, 1877), 261–77.

———. *Rodman the Keeper: Southern Sketches.* New York: D. Appleton, 1880.

———. "Sister St. Luke." *Galaxy,* XXIII (April, 1877), 489–506.

———. "The South Devil." *Atlantic Monthly,* XLV (February, 1880), 173–93.

———. "Up in the Blue Ridge." *Appleton's Journal,* n.s., V (August, 1878), 104–25.

———. "Up the Ashley and Cooper." *Harper's,* LII (December, 1875), 1–24.

SECONDARY WORKS

Aaron, Daniel. *The Unwritten War: American Writers and the Civil War.* New York: Alfred A. Knopf, 1973.

Adams, John R. *Harriet Beecher Stowe.* New York: Twayne Publishers, 1963.

American Literary Realism, I (Fall, 1968).

Anderson, Charles R. "Henry James's Fable of Carolina." *South Atlantic Quarterly,* LIV (1955), 249–57.

———. "James's Portrait of the Southerner." *American Literature,* XXVII (1955), 309–31.

Becker, George J. "Albion W. Tourgée: Pioneer in Social Criticism." *American Literature,* XIX (March, 1947), 59–72.

Benedict, Clare, ed. *Five Generations (1785–1923): Being Scattered Chapters from the History of the Cooper, Pomeroy, Woolson, and Benedict Families, with Extracts from the Letters and Journals, as well as Articles and Poems by Constance Fenimore Woolson.* 3 vols. London: Ellis, 1929–30.

Bisland, Elizabeth. *The Life and Letters of Lafcadio Hearn.* 2 vols. Boston: Houghton Mifflin, 1906.

Boatright, Mody C. "The American Myth Rides the Range: Owen Wister's Man on Horseback." *Southwest Review,* XXXVI (1951), 157–63.

Brooks, Van Wyck. "Henry James: The American Scene." *Dial,* LXXV (July, 1923), 29–42.

Brown, Sterling. *The Negro in American Fiction.* Albany: J. B. Lyon Press, 1937.

Buck, Paul H. *The Road to Reunion, 1865–1900.* Boston: Little, Brown, 1937.

Cash, W. J. *The Mind of the South.* New York: Alfred A. Knopf, 1941.

Coleman, Charles W., Jr. "The Recent Movement in Southern Literature." *Harper's,* LXXIV (May, 1887), 837–55.

Colvert, James B. "Views of Southern Character in Some Northern Novels." *Mississippi Quarterly,* XVIII (Spring, 1965), 59–68.

Craven, Avery. *Reconstruction: The Ending of the Civil War.* New York: Holt, Rinehart, and Winston, 1969.

Crozier, Alice C. *The Novels of Harriet Beecher Stowe.* New York: Oxford University Press, 1969.

Davidson, James. "The Post-Bellum Poor-White as Seen by J. W. De Forest." *Southern Folklore Quarterly,* XXIV (June, 1960), 101–108.

Dibble, Roy F. *Albion W. Tourgée.* New York: Lemcke and Buechner, 1921.

Doughty, Nanelia S. "Realistic Negro Characterization in Postbellum Fiction." *Negro American Literature Forum,* III (Summer, 1969), 57–62, 68.

Ealy, Marguerite, and Sanford E. Marovitz, eds. "Albion Winegar Tourgée (1838–1905)." *American Literary Realism,* VIII (Winter, 1975), 53–80.

Edel, Leon. *Henry James: The Middle Years, 1882–1895.* Philadelphia: J. B. Lippincott, 1962.

————. *Henry James: The Treacherous Years, 1895–1901.* Philadelphia: J. B. Lippincott, 1969.

Floan, Howard R. *The South in Northern Eyes, 1831 to 1861.* Austin: University of Texas Press, 1958.

Frost, O. W. "The Birth of Lafcadio Hearn." *American Literature,* XXIV (November, 1952), 372–77.

Gargano, James W. "A De Forest Interview." *American Literature,* XXIX (November, 1957), 320–22.

Gautier, Théophile. *One of Cleopatra's Nights and Other Fantastic Romances.* Translated by Lafcadio Hearn. New York: R. Worthington, 1882.

Gould, George M. *Concerning Lafcadio Hearn.* Philadelphia: George W. Jacobs, 1908.

————. "Human Colour Sense Considered." N.p., 1886.

Graff, Mary B. *Mandarin on the St. Johns*. Gainesville: University of Florida Press, 1953.

Green, Claud B. "The Rise and Fall of Local Color in Southern Literature." *Mississippi Quarterly*, XVIII (Winter 1964–65), 1–6.

Gross, Theodore. *Albion W. Tourgée*. New Haven: College and University Press, 1963.

———. "Albion W. Tourgée: Reporter of the Reconstruction." *Mississippi Quarterly*, XVI (Summer, 1963), 111–27.

———. "The Fool's Errand of Albion W. Tourgée." *Phylon*, XXIV (1963), 240–54.

Hagemann, E. R. "A Checklist of the Writings of John William De Forest (1826–1906)." *Studies in Bibliography*, VIII (1956), 185–94.

———. "John William De Forest and *The Galaxy*, Some Letters (1867–1872)." *Bulletin of the New York Public Library*, LIX (April, 1955), 175–94.

Haight, Gordon S. "Realism Defined: William Dean Howells." In *Literary History of the United States*, edited by Robert E. Spiller *et al.* Rev. ed. New York: Macmillan, 1963.

Harris, Joel Chandler. *Joel Chandler Harris: Editor and Essayist*. Edited by Julia Collier Harris. Chapel Hill: University of North Carolina Press, 1931.

Hayne, Paul Hamilton. *A Collection of Hayne Letters*. Edited by Daniel Morley McKeithan. Austin: University of Texas Press, 1944.

Hearn, Setsuko (Koizumi). *Reminiscences of Lafcadio Hearn*. Boston: Houghton Mifflin, 1918.

Holden, William Woods. *Third Annual Message of W. W. Holden, Governor of North Carolina*. Raleigh: J. W. Holden, 1870.

Howard, David. "The Bostonians." In *The Air of Reality: New Essays on Henry James*, edited by John Goode. London: Methuen and Company, 1972.

Howells, William Dean. Review of *Miss Ravenel's Conversion from Secession to Loyalty*, by John De Forest. *Atlantic Monthly*, XX (July, 1867), 120–22.

Hubbell, Jay B. *The South in American Literature, 1607–1900*. Durham: Duke University Press, 1954.

Kaplan, Sidney. "Albion W. Tourgée: Attorney for the Segregated." *Journal of Negro History*, XLIX (1964), 128–33.

Keller, Dean H. "A Checklist of the Writings of Albion W. Tourgée." *Studies in Bibliography*, XVIII (1965), 269–79.

Kern, John Dwight. *Constance Fenimore Woolson: Literary Pioneer.* Philadelphia: University of Pennsylvania Press, 1934.

Kunst, Arthur E. *Lafcadio Hearn.* New York: Twayne Publishers, 1969.

Lambert, Neal. "Owen Wister's Lin McLean: The Failure of the Vernacular Hero." *Western American Literature*, V (1970), 219–32.

———. "Owen Wister's Virginian: The Genesis of a Cultural Hero." *Western American Literature*, VI (1971), 99–107.

Leary, Lewis. "Lafcadio Hearn, 'One of our Southern Writers': A Footnote to Southern Literary History." In *Essays on American Literature in Honor of Jay B. Hubbell*, edited by Clarence Gohdes. Durham: Duke University Press, 1967.

Levy, Leo B. "Naturalism in the Making: De Forest's *Honest John Vane.*" *New England Quarterly*, XXXVII (March, 1964), 89–98.

Light, James F. *John William De Forest.* New Haven: College and University Press, 1965.

———. "John William De Forest (1826–1906)." *American Literary Realism*, I (Fall, 1967), 32–35.

Lively, Robert A. *Fiction Fights the Civil War: An Unfinished Chapter in the Literary History of the American People.* Chapel Hill: University of North Carolina Press, 1957.

Long, Robert Emmet. "The Society and the Masks: *The Blithedale Romance* and *The Bostonians.*" *Nineteenth Century Fiction*, XIX (September, 1964), 105–22.

McIntyre, Clara F. "J. W. De Forest, Pioneer Realist." *University of Wyoming Publications*, IX (August 31, 1942), 1–13.

McLean, Robert C. "*The Bostonians*: New England Pastoral." *Papers on Language and Literature*, VII (1971), 374–81.

McWilliams, Vera S. *Lafcadio Hearn.* Boston: Houghton Mifflin, 1946.

Martin, Jay. *Harvests of Change: American Literature 1865–1914.* Englewood Cliffs, N. J.: Prentice-Hall, 1967.

Mason, Julian. "Owen Wister and the South." *Southern Humanities Review*, VI (1972), 23–34.

———. "Owen Wister, Champion of Old Charleston." *Quarterly Journal of the Library of Congress*, XXIX (1972), 162–85.

Moore, Rayburn S. *Constance F. Woolson.* New Haven: College and University Press, 1963.

Morris, Wright. "Henry James's *The American Scene.*" *Texas Quarterly,* I (Summer-Autumn, 1958), 27–42.

Nye, Russell B. "Judge Tourgée and Reconstruction." *Ohio State Archaeological and Historical Quarterly,* L (April, 1941), 101–14.

O'Donnell, Thomas F. "De Forest, Van Petten, and Stephen Crane." *American Literature,* XXVII (January, 1956), 578–80.

Olenick, Monte M. "Albion W. Tourgée: Radical Republican Spokesman of the Civil War Crusade." *Phylon,* XXIII (Winter, 1962), 332–45.

Olsen, Otto H. "Albion W. Tourgée: Carpetbagger." *North Carolina Historical Review,* XL (Autumn, 1963), 434–54.

———. *Carpetbagger's Crusade: The Life of Albion Winegar Tourgée.* Baltimore: Johns Hopkins Press, 1965.

Osterweis, Rollin G. *The Myth of the Lost Cause, 1865–1900.* Hamden, Conn.: Shoe String Press, 1973.

Pattee, Fred Lewis. "Constance Fenimore Woolson and the South." *South Atlantic Quarterly,* XXXVIII (April, 1939), 130–41.

Perkins, P. D. and Ione. *Lafcadio Hearn: A Bibliography of His Writings.* Boston: Houghton Mifflin, 1934.

Rawlings, Marjorie Kinnan. "Regional Literature of the South." *College English,* I (February, 1940), 381–89.

Richardson, Lyon N. "Constance Fenimore Woolson, 'Novelist Laureate' of America " *South Atlantic Quarterly,* XXXIX (January, 1940), 18–36.

Rosenbaum, Sidonia C. "The Utopia of Lafcadio Hearn: Spanish America." *American Quarterly,* VI (Spring, 1954), 76–78.

Royall, William L. *A Reply to "A Fool's Errand, by One of the Fools."* New York: E. J. Hale and Son, 1880.

Rubin, Louis D., Jr. "Introduction to Part III, Southern Writing 1865–1920." In *Southern Writing, 1585–1920.* Edited by Richard Beale Davis, C. Hugh Holman, and Louis D. Rubin, Jr. New York: Odyssey Press, 1970.

Rush, N. Orwin. "Fifty Years of *The Virginian.*" *Papers of the Bibliographical Society of America,* XLVI (1952), 99–120.

Salvan, Albert J. "Lafcadio Hearn's Views on the Realism of Zola." *PMLA,* LXVII (December, 1952), 1163–67.

Shuman, R. Baird. "Hearn's Gift from the Sea: *Chita.*" *English Journal,* LVI (Spring, 1967), 822–27.

Simkins, Francis Butler. *A History of the South.* 3rd ed. New York: Alfred A. Knopf, 1963.

———. *Pitchfork Ben Tillman, South Carolinian.* Baton Rouge: Louisiana State University Press, 1944.

Sisson, Martha Howard. "A Bibliography of Lafcadio Hearn." *Bulletin of Bibliography,* XV (May-August, 1933; September-December, 1933; January-April, 1934; May-August, 1934), 6–7, 32–34, 55–56, 73–75.

Stevenson, Elizabeth. *Lafcadio Hearn.* New York: Macmillan, 1961.

Stone, Albert E., Jr. "Reading, Writing, and History: Best Novel of the Civil War." *American Heritage,* XIII (June, 1962), 84–88.

Taylor, William R. *Cavalier and Yankee: The Old South and American National Character.* New York: Harper and Row, 1961.

Tinker, Edward Larocque. *Lafcadio Hearn's American Days.* New York: Dodd, Mead, 1924.

Trelease, Allen W. *White Terror: The Ku Klux Klan Conspiracy and Southern Reconstruction.* New York: Harper and Row, 1971.

Trilling, Lionel. *The Opposing Self: Nine Essays in Criticism.* New York: Viking Press, 1955.

Wagenknecht, Edward. *Harriet Beecher Stowe: The Known and the Unknown.* New York: Oxford University Press, 1965.

White, G. Edward. *The Eastern Establishment and the Western Experience: The West of Frederic Remington, Theodore Roosevelt, and Owen Wister.* New Haven: Yale University Press, 1968.

Wilson, Edmund. *Patriotic Gore: Studies in the Literature of the American Civil War.* Rev. ed. New York: Oxford University Press, 1966.

Wilson, Forrest. *Crusader in Crinoline: The Life of Harriet Beecher Stowe.* New York: J. B. Lippincott, 1941.

Woodward, C. Vann. *The Burden of Southern History.* Rev. ed. Baton Rouge: Louisiana State University Press, 1968.

———. *Origins of the New South, 1877–1913.* Vol. IX of *A History of the South,* edited by Wendell Holmes Stephenson and E. Merton Coulter, 10 vols. Baton Rouge: Louisiana State University Press, 1971.

Yu, Beongcheon. *An Ape of Gods: The Art and Thought of Lafcadio Hearn.* Detroit: Wayne State University Press, 1964.

Index

The American Scene (James): discussed, 123–29; and Lady Baltimore, 112, 125, 126; mentioned, 136
Atlantic Monthly, xix–xx, 54

Beecher, the Reverend Lyman, 2–3
Benedict, Clare, 56
Bisland, Elizabeth, 78–79
blacks: in fiction, xviii, xix; in Stowe's work, 4–5, 12–13, 14–16; stereotyped, 19, 47, 48; in De Forest's work, 24, 44, 47–48, 59, 115; in Tourgée's work, 38, 40–42, 46, 47, 115; in Woolson's work, 59, 60–61; in Hearn's work, 81, 82; in Wister's work, 113, 115–16; mentioned, xi, xvii. See also education of blacks
The Bostonians (James), 129–34, 136
Brett, George, 111
Bricks Without Straw (Tourgée), 34, 35, 37n, 39–42, 51–52
Butler, Major Pierce, 110

Cable, George Washington, 77
carpetbaggers, xiii, xviii. See also Reconstruction
Cassimati, Rose, 74
Century Magazine, 54
Charleston, S.C.: Wister's idealization of, 100, 110, 113, 122; Wister in, 109–11; Wister and James in, 111–12, 122, 123; Crum incident in, 116–18; James in, 126–28, 138; mentioned, 56, 126

Chita (Hearn), 87, 89–95, 138; sources of, 77, 83
cowboy hero, 101–104, 108–109
Crane, Stephen, 26
"A Creole Courtyard" (Hearn), 83–84
Crum incident, 116–18

De Forest, John William: reform fiction of, xx, 23, 26, 42, 67; and use of South idealized, xx, 44, 52–53, 66–67, 84, 88; life of, 23–24; and Tourgée, 23, 32, 42–43, 52–53; as realistic writer, 24–26; and Woolson, 58, 64–65, 69, 72–73; and Hearn, 81, 86, 88; and Wister, 115; The History of the Indians of Connecticut, 23; Oriental Acquaintance, 23; European Acquaintance, 23; A Volunteer's Adventures, 24; A Union Officer in the Reconstruction, 24 and n, 44–46; Miss Ravenel's Conversion from Secession to Loyalty, 25, 27–31, 47–51, 69, 137, 138; Kate Beaumont, 25, 31–32, 46–49, 59; The Bloody Chasm, 25; "Rum Creeters is Women," 25n; "The Great American Novel," 26–27; mentioned, 34, 54, 104
De Leon, Edwin, xx
Democratic party, xvii, xviii
Dred (Stowe), 10–17

East Angels (Woolson), 61, 70–73
easterners, 99–100
East-West dichotomy: in Wister's work,

151